Flyfishing Tips, Techniques & Strategies

from the Experts

Flyfishing Tips, Techniques & Strategies

from the Experts

Paul N. Fling &
Donald L. Puterbaugh

with Phil Camera,
Al Diem, Jerry Gibbs &
Joan Salvato Wulff

Sterling Publishing Co., Inc.
New York

To Steve, Mace, Lance, and Slaton—the shack pack.

Other Works by the Authors:

The Basic Manual of Fly-Tying

Expert Fly-Tying

Fly-Fisherman's Primer

Thanks to Joan Wulff and Stackpole Books, Mechanicsburg, Pennsylvania, for permission to use excerpts from *Joan Wulff's Fly Fishing: Expert Advice from a Woman's Perspective* (1991).

Library of Congress Cataloging-in-Publication Data

Fling, Paul N.
    Flyfishing tips, techniques & strategies from the experts / Paul
N. Fling & Donald L. Puterbaugh with Phil Camera . . . [et al.].
        p.   cm.
    Includes index.
    ISBN 0-8069-4255-X
    1. Fly fishing.   I. Puterbaugh, Donald L.   II. Title.
SH456.F548   1997
    799.1'24—dc21   97–44356
                                                                 CIP

10 9 8 7 6 5 4 3 2 1

Published by Sterling Publishing Company, Inc.
387 Park Avenue South, New York, N.Y. 10016
© 1998 by Paul Fling and Donald L. Puterbaugh
Distributed in Canada by Sterling Publishing
c/o Canadian Manda Group, One Atlantic Avenue, Suite 105
Toronto, Ontario, Canada M6K 3E7
Distributed in Great Britain and Europe by Cassell PLC
Wellington House, 125 Strand, London WC2R 0BB, England
Distributed in Australia by Capricorn Link (Australia) Pty Ltd.
P.O. Box 6651, Baulkham Hills, Business Centre, NSW 2153, Australia
Printed in Hong Kong

Sterling ISBN 0-8069-4255-X

Contents

Preface

Much of the fascination of flyfishing stems from the fact that the successful flyfisher must have several skills that are well developed: accurate casting, an ability to read the water, and a basic understanding of aquatic entomology.

A few hours spent practicing your casting can develop your skill sufficiently. There are myriad books that will tell you all you need to know about reading water and take you as deep into aquatic entomology as you want to delve. In addition to these requisite skills, though, expert flyfishers have developed a repertoire of tricks and techniques, primarily through experience, which provide them with the additional bits and pieces that make their time astream more effective. Many times, the individuals aren't even aware of the how or why of what they are doing—they simply do what works.

This book is an attempt to assemble some of these subtleties in a single place so that you can avoid the trial-and-error effort that learning by experience requires. Very few—perhaps, none—are secrets that only the contributor has stumbled across. Many, in fact, were suggested by more than one of the contributors, which really shouldn't be surprising. After all, none of us has sole ownership of the ability to come up with a workable solution to a common problem. Therefore, even though we've identified the individuals who provided the specific technique or tip, we don't mean to suggest that they are the only ones who have found the solution, or even that the idea is original with them.

Someone once said, only half-jokingly, that an expert is someone more than fifty miles from home with a tray of slides. The truth is that few of us consider ourselves or those close around us experts. After all, we've seen their foibles and are painfully aware of our own. All of our contributors would vehemently deny being experts; that moniker implies a complete command of the knowledge and skills used in flyfishing, and they're all experienced enough to know there's still so much more to learn. Maybe that's what makes each of them an expert. Although not laying claim to the title for themselves, each of them probably wouldn't hesitate to classify the others in that category. We certainly consider all of them experts.

We hope you find the tips assembled here helpful. If just one of these offerings turns a poor day of fishing into a good day, a good day into a great day, or saves a trip for you, our efforts will have been successful.

Acknowledgments

We are deeply indebted to our contributors, all of whom provided such good material and delivered it on time. Each of you has earned our heartfelt thanks. A special thank-you to Joan Wulff, who not only provided material, but also graciously allowed extensive use of material from her wonderful book, *Joan Wulff's Fly Fishing: Expert Advice From a Woman's Perspective* (Stackpole Books, Mechanicsburg, Pennsylvania, 1991).

An acknowledgment is due *Field and Stream Magazine,* New York, which first published articles of ours under the titles "Simplified Fly Selection" (June, 1991) and "A Fly Fisherman's Troubleshooting Guide" (March, 1993), from which some of the material herein is adapted. Working with them is always a treat.

Charles Nurnberg and the staff at Sterling have led us through this putting together of a book for the fourth time now. Their sage advice and great editing (thanks once again, Isabel Stein) have always been sound. Most important, though, they exhibit patience above and beyond the call.

And of course, to Pam and Polly, for putting up with the book-writing process so graciously.

About the Contributors

Phil Camera is well known throughout the flyfishing industry as an innovator of fly design and materials application, as well as an expert flyfisherman. He is the author of *Fly Tying with Synthetics* and has flyfished throughout the United States and Europe, giving seminars and field-testing his products. He devoted years of experimentation to the development of his Larva Lace synthetic tying material, which has become a standard item in the fly-tyer's arsenal. In addition to providing hundreds of flytying clinics, he has become a fixture at fishing expositions, where he demonstrates the versatility of synthetic materials. His two videos, *Freshwater Synthetics* and *Realistic Saltwater Synthetics,* have been featured in the *Hooked on Fly Tying* series. Phil makes his home in Woodland Park, Colorado.

Al Diem began his fishing career using an antenna from a World War II Sherman tank. He has progressed from that humble beginning to become a flyfisherman of stature. Al has flyfished throughout the world for many species, including those found in the saltwater domains. His real passion, though, is for trout and Atlantic salmon. He is the creator of the Aqua

Designs line of fishing wear for the serious fisherman. Al makes his home in upstate Vermont.

Jerry Gibbs has been the fishing editor for *Outdoor Life* magazine since 1973. He writes a column for *Salt Water Flyfishing* magazine and is a regular contributor to other sportfishing publications. He's the author or co-author of many angling books, including a collection of short stories: *Steel Barbs, Wild Waters.* Gibbs has been sportfishing contributor to *Encyclopedia Britannica* and a consultant to the fishing tackle industry. He has won top honors from the Outdoor Writers Association of America, received awards for excellence in craft and service from the U.S. tackle industry, and has been inducted into the Fresh Water Fishing Hall of Fame. Jerry has fished across the U.S. and Canada, in Europe, the Caribbean, Central and South America, Russia, New Zealand, and Australia.

Joan Wulff is the author of *Joan Wulff's Fly Casting Techniques, Joan Wulff's Fly Fishing: Expert Advice From a Woman's Perspective,* and *Joan Wulff's Fly Casting Accuracy.* She writes a casting column for *Fly Rod & Reel* magazine, where she is also the editor at large. She operates the Wulff School of Fly Fishing and has recently begun offering schools for casting instructors. Joan is a consultant to the R. L. Winston Rod company, which introduced the Joan Wulff Favorite to its line in 1996. She has appeared in numerous films, videos, and television specials and is the recipient of many awards, including Federation of Flyfishers Woman of the Year, Fly Rod and Reel Angler of the Year, American Sportfishing Association Woman of the Year, and the NAFTA Lifetime Achievement Award.

chapter one

Equipment

The Basics

There's a tremendous variety of equipment marketed for the flyfisher; every year the manufacturers strive to come up with additional items that we'll all decide we must have. "Surely, that new-generation graphite rod, precision-machined reel, or high-tech line will cure all my casting ills....Those new waders and studded-sole boots will let me wade more safely and reach spots that I had to pass up last year." And so it goes, right down to the new tippet material that is two-tenths of a pound stronger than last year's.

Well, it is exciting to get new equipment and, in many cases, there is some advantage over the older stuff we're using, but, whatever the new item under consideration, the basic requirements for a well-balanced outfit remain the same.

Most newcomers to flyfishing assume that the first equipment choice they need to make is which rod to buy. Although that may be the most important decision they'll need to make, it's not the first one. You might find just the sweetest, best-feeling rod in the fly shop, but if it casts a 3-weight line and you're going to be fishing for king salmon on big, windy, Alaskan rivers, it's not the right choice.

To make a sound choice of a fly rod, you'll first need to determine what line size the rod will need to handle. That decision is based on the species of fish you'll be pursuing and the kind of water you'll be fishing the majority of the time.

Line Weight, Taper, and Type

Taper, line weight, and type are identified by a line code printed on the box and spool that come with the line. The code has 3 parts. *The first letter or letters* specifies the taper or shape of the line: level (L), double taper (DT), weight forward (WF), or shooting taper (ST). *The number* designates the line weight, and *the last letter or letters* shows the type of the line: floating (F), sinking (S), or sink-tip (F/S). For example, WF6F breaks down to: WF = weight forward; 6 = 6-weight; F = floating line.

Weight

The line weight, indicated by the number in the line code, is based on the weight of the first 30 feet (9.2 m) of the line (in our example, 152 to 168 grains for the 6-weight line).

The choice of line weight is the first step in putting together a flyfishing outfit, because fly rods are built so they will efficiently cast a line of a particular weight. A rod designed to cast a 4-weight line very effectively won't be stiff enough to handle the extra weight of, say, a 6-weight line. Your rod choice, therefore, is dependent on the line weight you decide to use. The choice of line weight *should* be dictated by the particular fishing conditions that you will most often encounter when you go to the stream. The fact is, though, this choice is more often made based on what everyone else chooses to use, whether that's really the best choice or not.

The trend in recent years, with the advent of even lighter weight, generation-three and -four graphite rods, has been towards the use of lighter lines. The new, small-diameter rods are very powerful. There is certainly some validity in choosing a rod that casts a lighter line, as such a rod is lighter and less tiring to use. Using a heavier line-weight outfit throughout a full day of fishing on a small river represents a tremendous waste of energy; you'll be much more arm weary at the end of the day than if you had used a lighter outfit. On the other hand, if you will be spending much or most of your time on waters where a significant wind is the norm, you will expend more energy in a day casting that 4- or 5-weight line into the wind than you would if you had used a 6- or 7-weight line-and-rod combination. The heavier line will bore through the air more easily than the lightweight line and, even given the extra weight of the heavier outfit, your total energy consumption will be less.

Most serious flyfishers own several rods, which handle a range of line weights. Surely some of the variety owned is simply because it's a pleasure to have and handle fine rods. But, if you are going to fish under a wide spectrum of conditions or for a variety of species, there's sound reason for having a selection of rods handling different line weights to match those conditions.

Taper

Fly lines are built in four basic shapes, called tapers (Fig. 1). Level lines (L in the code) are of equal diameter from end to end. They simply cannot be cast with efficiency. You shouldn't even consider buying a level fly line, as even the "experts" would have a hard time casting one.

Double-taper (DT) lines are cigar-shaped, with a heavy center section. They taper equally to either end. Double-taper lines cast efficiently and are a good choice for an all-around line. Since each half of the line is identical to the other, the line can be reversed when one end gets worn; therefore, double-taper lines will have a longer usable life than other types.

Weight-forward (WF) lines are similar to double-taper lines, but in the weight-forward, the heavier center

1. Three tapers of line. (Not shown, shooting taper.)

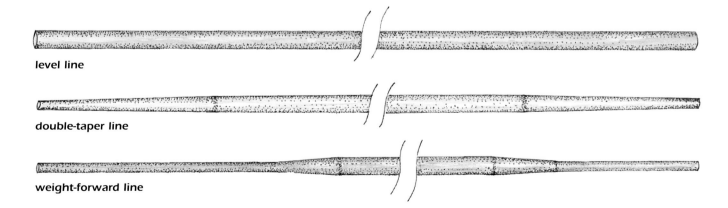

level line

double-taper line

weight-forward line

section is moved forward towards one end of the line. This allows you to get enough weight to cast efficiently with less line past the rod tip. The weight-forward line is the most popular line shape but can't, of course, be reversed since the shape isn't symmetrical like the double-taper line.

The shooting-taper (ST) line is a special-use line, only 30 feet long, which is used for situations that demand long-distance casting.

A large variety of other special taper lines have been introduced by manufacturers over the years: rocket taper, bass taper, steelhead taper, pike taper, bonefish taper, tarpon taper, distance taper, nymph taper, wind taper, and on and on. Each of these involves shifting the heavier section of a weight-forward line further forward or back, but the first 30 feet still weighs the same for a given line weight. These specialty lines do provide some advantages for specific types of fishing. For 90 percent of us, 90 percent of the time, though, a simple weight-forward (WF) line will do everything we need on the trout stream.

Line Type

The major types of lines are floating, sinking, and floating/sinking (sink-tip). The entire length of a floating line is constructed so that it will float on the surface of the water. The density of a sinking line is controlled by the manufacturer to ensure that its entire length will sink. A sink-tip line is a combination of the two, designed so

that the first 10 or 20 feet (3 or 6 m) will sink while the rest of the line will float. Let's take a look at each line type and its application.

Floating lines are designated *F* in the line code. A floating line is used for all dry-fly fishing, most nymph or wet-fly fishing, and for fishing streamers where great depth isn't necessary. A major advantage of a floating line is that the entire line remains on the surface of the water and is thus more easily controlled, because you can see the effect of the current on the line. It is also much easier to pick up the line from the water at the start of the backcast. The floating line is the appropriate choice for at least 90 percent of flyfishing situations; it should be your choice for a basic outfit.

Full sinking lines are designated *S* in the line code. Sinking lines are used in those cases where you need to consistently present your fly very deep in a stream or lake. They are advantageous in some situations where a streamer, wet fly, or nymph must travel right down on the bottom in very deep and/or fast-moving water. There are instances where that is the only presentation that will take fish, but those instances aren't too common; you're not likely to use a sinking line very often. A disadvantage of a sinking line is that you can't pick up the line from the water to begin your backcast; you have to strip nearly all of the line in before you can start casting. Sinking lines are made in a variety of sink rates, which are expressed in inches per second.

Sink-tip lines are abbreviated *F/S* (floating/sinking). They are typically available with either a 10- or 20-foot section at the end that sinks. Like full-sinking lines, sink-tip lines are available with various sink rates for the sinking tip section. These are the second most commonly used lines, because the sinking tip section is long enough to get the fly down into the depths of the stream for fishing deep streamers, wet flies, or nymphs, but most of the line remains floating on the surface, where you can see and control it and pick it up easily for the backcast.

Your line is perhaps the most important piece of your equipment, because your ability to cast efficiently is dependent on its functioning properly. Good fly lines are expensive, but you're better off saving a few dollars by buying a less expensive rod or reel than skimping on the fly line.

For the one-rod angler, our recommendation is a weight-forward or double-taper, floating 5- or 6-weight line (WF5F, WF6F, DT5F, or DT6F). Any of these is a good compromise: light enough to avoid being tiring to cast, yet linked with a rod that has enough power to handle windy conditions and long casts.

Rod Material and Length

Graphite has become the standard rod material in recent years. Graphite rods have the advantage of being very light while possessing tremendous strength. They are also very effective casting tools as they dampen out oscillations quickly and transfer energy from the rod to the line efficiently. Because graphite rods can be mass produced, their cost covers a wide range, from very inexpensive up to several hundred dollars. Even the most expensive graphite rods, however, are priced at one-half to one-third of the other available rod material, cane (bamboo).

Split cane was the first rod material that was truly efficient for casting a fly. The construction of a cane rod requires a great amount of meticulous handwork; consequently, they are very expensive. Cane rods are heavier than graphite for a given rod length and line weight and aren't quite as efficient as graphite is at transferring the casting energy into the fly line. They aren't nearly as durable as graphite rods, and they require more careful use. On the other hand, they possess a gentleness in their action that is unique. Additionally, because they are handcrafted and constructed of a natural material, they are beautiful tools that instill real pride of ownership. If money is no object or you simply must have the top of the line, a cane rod will suit you very well. For most of us, though, a graphite rod is the likely choice.

Although a couple of ounces difference in rod weight doesn't seem like much, when that ounce or two is multiplied by the several thousand casting strokes we make in a day of fishing, the effect on the angler is significant. Because a graphite rod built for casting a given line weight is lighter than a rod built of cane, the angler has the option of using a longer graphite rod. There is, of course, a trade-off. The longer rod means that the weight of the fly line is at the end of a longer lever when you are casting; consequently it applies more force into your hand and arm. This isn't a major factor, though, and the most common lengths are now 8½ and 9 feet.

A longer rod has several advantages in most situations. The extra length puts the backcast higher above the water and surrounding terrain, you have a longer reach and can mend the line more effectively, and you can cover more water when using a tight-line nymphing technique.

Our recommendation for an all-around rod is an 8½- or 9-foot graphite rod casting a 5- or 6-weight line.

Reels

Fly reels come in four basic types: automatic, single-action, double-action, and multiplier.

An automatic fly reel weighs three or four times as much as a single- or double-action reel, has very limited line capacity, and simply has no place in modern trout fishing.

The difference between a single-action and a double-action fly reel is that the single-action reel applies the same amount of resistance when you are stripping line from the reel as when you are reeling it in. The double-action reel applies more resistance when you are stripping out line (i.e., a fish is running line off the reel) than when you retrieve it. Since the drag that a fly reel applies to the line is very light, you would be hard pressed to notice the difference between retrieving line against the same drag resistance (single-action) or retrieving it against slightly less resistance, as with a double-action reel. It just doesn't matter much; most manufacturers don't even use the classifications.

Multiplier reels are similar to single- or double-action reels, but with the addition of a gear train that allows the spool to turn more than one revolution for each turn of the reel handle (usually 2:1 or 3:1). The addition of the gears requires that the reel be somewhat larger and heavier than the same reel in a single- or double-action model. Their supposed advantage is that if a large fish turns and runs towards you, you can retrieve line faster, to avoid giving the fish any slack. The few really large fish (salmon) that I have had turn and run back upriver towards me were coming much too fast to keep the slack out with any reel, however.

In the last few years, the market has become full of high-quality, high-dollar reels. Although they all tout their individual features, the fact is that there is really very little difference among them in a given price range. The major difference between the mid-range-priced reel and the very expensive is in the fit and finish. The top-end reels are machined to very close tolerances: a 6X tippet (.005 inch) won't fit between the spool and frame. They have exceptionally smooth drags and are finished like fine pieces of jewelry. They are delightful to own and use. They do, however, represent overkill for the pursuit of trout. Unless you're after salmon, steelhead, or saltwater species, you simply won't gain any advantage in your day-to-day fishing with one of these high-end beauties—but they sure are nice!

The other extreme, a cheap reel, will be onerous. Its extra weight will completely negate the advantage that you gained by buying a lightweight graphite rod. You'll be able to get not only your tippet but a part of your fly line between the spool and frame, and the reel will probably quit working just when you need it the most. Don't buy a cheap reel; there are plenty of really good reels in the middle price range and they are worth the small extra cost over the cheap ones.

A given make and model of reel is usually available in a range of sizes, to accommodate different line weights. You should select one that is made for the line weight you are using. This will ensure that there is room for the line and a reasonable amount of backing, while keeping the size and weight to a minimum so that the rod and reel are in balance.

Leaders and Tippets

Whether to use a knotted or knotless leader is strictly a matter of personal choice. Either one will do an efficient job of transferring the necessary energy from the fly line to the fly at the completion of the cast. Either a 7½- or 9-foot 4X leader will work fine as the starting point for most trout fishing. It's not too often that you need a heavier leader than 4X. Usually, if you need to step down to a smaller size, it's also advantageous to lengthen the leader; both needs are satisfied by adding tippet material (level monofilament) to your basic leader. There are exceptions, such as when fishing very small midges (#22 and smaller). In that case, it makes sense to begin with a 9-foot or 12-foot 6X or 7X leader.

You need to carry tippet material in sizes 3X through 7X to cover the full range of possible needs on the stream. Having this range of sizes, you can adjust your basic leader to meet any conditions without changing the leader itself. The basic rule for tippet size is that the tippet X designator should be equal to the fly size divided by 4. For example, if you're using a #16 size fly, your tippet should be 4X. There are many exceptions to the rule, as we try to balance the need for delicacy of presentation against the practicality of casting the fly accurately. We'll look at some of these exceptions when we discuss tips and techniques.

Fly Vests

Unlike the bank or boat angler, the flyfisher can't carry around a tackle box full of equipment. It takes both hands to flycast, and places to set down a tackle box are few and far between out in the river. Yet there are a variety of things the flyfisher needs to have available. A fly vest has been the traditional method of carrying along all those needs for the past 60 years or so. Chest packs (or fore and aft packs) have become popular in the last few years. Both the traditional vest and the newer packs provide a place to carry along the needed items without hindering your ability to wade or cast. We all seem to be drawn to vests with the maximum number of pockets. Having enough pockets to carry the necessities with you certainly is important. Having too many pockets, however, tends to lead to accumulating too much stuff; as a result, the same person who agonized for days over the choice between two rods with a 1/4-ounce difference in weight is often out in the stream lugging around 15 or 20 pounds of equipment.

Of more importance than the sheer number of pockets in a vest is their size and location. If you already have your fly boxes, take the largest one with you when shopping for a vest. You don't want to get home and then find that your boxes won't fit comfortably in the pockets. Try the vest on and then see how easily you can open, close, and get items into and out of the pockets. If there's any difficulty at all in the store, you can bet it will be twice as tough when you're standing in tumbling water with your rod tucked under one arm.

Most vests are cut large enough to fit over cold-weather clothing, but make sure that's the case. The less-expensive models sometimes are cut a little smaller than the top-of-the-line models. You'll probably want a rear pocket that closes, one large enough to carry a rain parka. A rear pocket that closes, either with a zipper or Velcro strip, won't collect debris from the trees, weeds, and brush along the bank or act as a catch basin for rain-water running down your back.

The "must" items in your vest include: clippers or scissors of some sort for cutting leader material and trimming knots; forceps for removing hooks from the fish; tippet material; fly boxes; fly floatant; desiccant; leader sink; split shot or lead strips for weighting your leader; strike indicators for nymph fishing; a hook-sharpening stone or file; insect repellent; sunscreen; safety pin; rain jacket; and polarized sunglasses (I wear my good ones for everything, including fishing, but keep an inexpensive pair permanently in my vest as a backup).

There's no limit (beyond what you can carry) to the other items you might include in or on your vest. A stream thermometer, trout stomach pump, permanent marking pens (for changing fly colors), knot tyers, spare reel, spare spool (with sink-tip or sinking line), landing net, line cleaner, leader straightener, angler's clip-on flashlight, magnifier, fingerless gloves, insect-collecting seine, and last week's half-eaten lunch are only a few of the things I've found in my vest at one time or another.

Waders

The ability to move around in the stream is absolutely necessary to the flyfisher. On many steams, the only way to get room for your backcast is to be out in the river, so that you can cast in the open area up and down the stream. Just as important, the option of changing your position in the stream allows you to cast a shorter line, which increases your accuracy and lets you reach spots with your cast that wouldn't be reachable from the shore. It also allows you the opportunity to cross the river or stream to fish the other side. There are several viable options as to what type of waders you may choose, but you do need to have waders of some sort. If you think making a rod choice was difficult…

The first consideration regarding waders is the type of sole they have. If your fishing takes you into streams whose bottoms are sand or mud, you need molded rubber lug-type soles on your waders. More likely, though, you'll need felt soles, because the places where trout live are usually rocky. Felt soles grip through the algae on the rocks, whereas rubber soles slide right off. You can also buy felt-sole waders that have tungsten studs embedded in the felt. Those really give you good traction, but they're expensive and sure do a number on car carpeting and floor mats, as you'll see if you are going to be driving from spot to spot along the river. Another alternative is to buy studded wading sandals that fit over your regular wading shoes or boots.

The second consideration is whether to buy boots or waders with an integral boot (called boot-foot waders) or stocking-foot waders and separate wading boots that fit over the foot end of the waders. Both types have their advantages and disadvantages.

Boot-foot styles are much quicker to put on and take off. Since they are all one piece, you're not going to arrive at the river only to discover that you forgot your wading boots or only brought one along. Their biggest disadvantage is their loose fit; since the boots can't open up for your feet, they have to be large enough for your feet to slip into them. That means that your feet will slip around in them once they are on, and you won't be as agile in the stream.

Since stocking-foot waders require a separate boot, the boot can open up to admit your foot and then be tightened with laces or Velcro straps. They fit comfortably. Your feet don't move around inside the boots, so you can wade much better. On the down side, stocking-foot waders and their accompanying boots are considerably more bother to put on and take off than boot-foot waders are.

You also need to decide whether you are going to buy your waders in a chest-high, waist-high, or hip-high model. Obviously, the chest-high version allows you to wade deeper and is less likely to ship water if you stumble. Chest-high waders sure are hot in the summer, though.

The waist-high model lets you wade about as deep as you probably should in most streams, and they're cooler than chest-high waders. Waist-high waders don't allow much room for errors in judgment as to water depth, however. A friend of ours who had worn chest waders for years was quite proud of his new waist-high neoprenes. I'll admit that on that hot August day I was rather envious, until he sat down on a large rock in the river where he often perched for a rest. He was quite dry in chest waders, but the water ran a couple of inches over his new waist-highs. He really *was* cool for the next hour or so—all the way to his crotch.

Hip waders (also called hippers or hip boots) are by far the most comfortable style to wear. They're the easiest to get off and on and the least encumbering of the styles. On some streams they are all that you need, but in the main they practically guarantee that you'll get wet before the day's over. You just can't wade deep enough in most streams in hippers, so you're constantly pushing their limits, and any misstep is going to slosh water over the top. They severely restrict where you can wade; that restricts your ability to reach a lot of productive water on most streams and rivers. They're wonderful to wear in those few places where they are truly all you need, but they probably shouldn't be your only wading gear.

The last decision regarding waders is which type of material to choose. There are three main choices: coated nylon, neoprene, or a breathable waterproof material such as Gore-tex. Coated nylon is lighter and cooler than neoprene, but bulkier. Neoprene fits like a glove and is more flexible, but it's hotter. Breathable waders are extremely light, allow any moisture collecting inside to pass through to the outside, and are softly flexible. They're the most comfortable waders, but they are very expensive.

Waders made from each type of material are available in a choice of thicknesses. In all cases, the thinner materials are more flexible, cooler, and more comfortable. The thicker materials, however, are considerably more durable and resistant to tears and punctures. The extra warmth they offer is an advantage in some seasons.

You could, of course, avoid the decision-making by buying each of the three heights of waders in both felt- and rubber-sole models; in boot-foot and stocking-foot styles; in coated nylon, neoprene, and breathable materials; and in heavyweight and lightweight fabrics. Seventy-two pair and you're all set!

Clothing

At first look, the clothing we wear when flyfishing doesn't seem too important. There are, however, a number of things to be considered. Probably the most important is that your clothing needs to blend into the background. Trout *do* see out of the water and *do* have color vision, so a bright red shirt or hat in their field of vision would certainly touch an instinctive chord that says there's something out there that doesn't fit the environment—translation, DANGER!

The ultimate for blending into the background is a new line of shirts, hats, pants, shorts, rain jackets, and vests called Aqua Design— camouflage, if you will, for the flyfisher. The fabric used for the clothing is printed with a pattern that is a computer-enhanced image of actual photos taken from under the water looking into different backgrounds. There are patterns that represent the trout's view of sandy, open environments; blue skies; rocky shores and clay banks; forested, brushy shorelines; and dark, rocky, canyonlike backgrounds.

We've all been made aware of the increased risk of skin cancer that comes with exposure to the sun. Common sense, it would seem, tells us that we need to wear long-sleeved shirts and hats (and sunscreen, as well) to protect us from the sun's rays. Long-sleeved shirts with Swiss tabs, which allow you to roll the sleeves up when the sun's not out, are a great idea.

Not only should you wear a hat for protection from the sun, but you really should wear one to protect your head, ears, and attached appendages from errant flies. There's never been a year that I didn't hook my hat at least once (usually the result of gusting wind, you understand). If the hook hadn't been buried in my hat, it'd be in my person somewhere. No thanks!

We've seen many times when the trout's feeding activity increased noticeably when it started to rain, especially in a light sprinkle. There will be times when you will want to keep fishing during a rain. A rain jacket will make that time much more comfortable. A rain jacket should be lightweight and fold up small enough to fit in the rear pocket of your vest. A hood to keep the rain from running down your neck is nice. It's also nice that the hood has a bill to keep the rainwater from running down your nose. (Get out of the river if there's lightning, however; that graphite rod is a 9-foot lightning rod!)

In cool weather, the best approach is to layer clothing so that you can be flexible as the temperature and your activity level change during the day.

Your rain jacket will also serve to shed a harsh wind and can increase your comfort level greatly on a cold day.

Although not exactly clothing, polarized sunglasses are an absolute necessity when flyfishing, so we'll include them here. They cut through the glare on the surface of the water so you can see your fly. They also allow you to see into the water, which is a great aid not only in spotting fish, but in wading.

Just as important, though, they provide protection for your eyes from that hook on the end of your leader. The thought of burying a hook anywhere in

your body is unpleasant, but the thought of a hook in the eye is enough to cause a shudder. Wear glasses!

Equipment Tips and Techniques

Stringing the rod. A young student of ours and I had parked our cars. He was stringing up his rod while I was fumbling through my carryall bag, loading up my fly boxes, and checking that I had plenty of tippet material, floatant, and all those things that I expect a beginner to lack. I noticed

2. Stringing the rod.

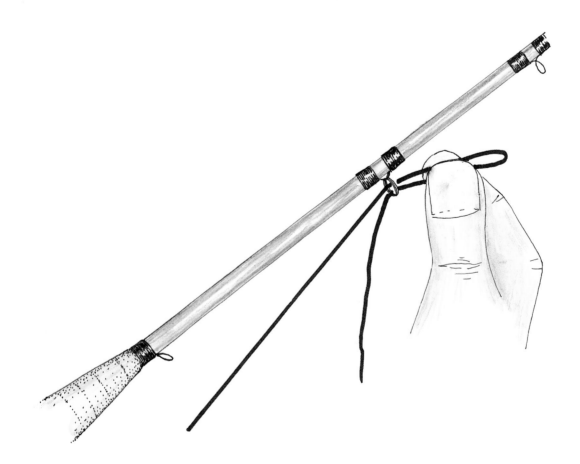

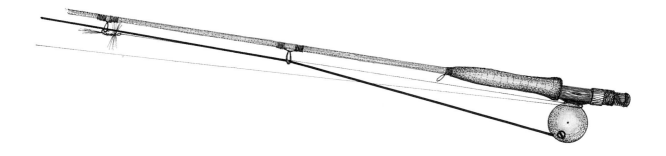

after some time that he was still stringing up his rod, so I went over and asked what the problem was. "I've got this thing almost strung four times now and every time I've dropped the leader before getting to the top guide, and it falls clear back out on the ground," he said.

This is a common situation that a lot of flyfishers experience. The solution is easy: instead of passing the leader up through the guides, simply pull some line off the reel and double it into a loop. Pass this loop up through the guides. If you do drop it, the loop will open up and catch in the next guide, instead of falling back down through all of the guides (Fig. 2).

Storing your leader. You will often find that your leader is longer than your rod. This presents a problem when you need to reel in the line to move to another spot. If you hook

your fly in the neat little hook-keeper that the rod-maker put on the rod just above the reel seat and wind up the line, the knot that joins the leader and the line will be inside the tip guide. When you get to the next spot and try to pull out some line to begin casting, it will be a struggle to get the knot back out through the tip guide.

Instead of hooking the fly in the hook-keeper, wrap the leader around the back of the reel and hook the fly on one of the guides, so you can reel up the slack without pulling the line/leader knot back inside the tip guide (Fig. 3).

Adding tippet. I generally use a knotless tapered leader, and I sometimes find that I get so caught up in the fishing that I don't bother to add new tippet to my leader to replace what I have used up changing flies. Before long, I've worked my way up the taper to

3. Wrap the line behind the reel to keep the leader knot outside the tip guide.

where the diameter is two or three sizes bigger than the original tippet. Now, I've got to stop and add several sections of decreasing tippet sizes to get back down to the original diameter.

I noticed that I didn't have the problem when I used a knotted leader. The knot that connects the final tippet section to the one above it reminded me to add tippet. Now when I tie on a new tapered leader, I add a foot or so of the same size tippet material as the end of the leader. When I get to the knot, I'm reminded that I need to add tippet before I start using up the leader.

Semi-permanent butt section. You can avoid the problem of the line/leader knot getting hung up in the tip guide by using either an internal nail knot or an epoxy splice. Both of these, however, are rather difficult to tie on the stream when you need to change a leader. An easy solution is to tie the internal nail knot or make the epoxy splice at home. Then, the first time you need to change your leader, cut it off so that you have 12 to 18 inches (30 to 46 cm) of the butt still attached to the fly line. Now all you need to do to change your leader is tie the butt of the new leader to this section, using your normal barrel knot or surgeon's knot. We generally don't change the entire leader very often, so that permanent butt section will probably last you for a whole season.

Alternative floatants. There you are: the trout are on a feeding spree, taking adult insects off the surface. Your fingers quiver with excitement as you select just the right dry fly from your fly box and tie it on. You reach in your vest pocket for your fly floatant—and it's not there. You fumble through all the pockets before you accept that *it's just not there.* Your new fly floats well enough on the first drift but barely stays on top during the next one, and after each couple of drifts you have to change flies to get a good drift. You may have the solution in your vest in the form of lip balm. The stuff has a wax-and-petroleum base. Both ingredients are waterproof, and that's the idea behind a floatant. We don't advocate replacing your regular floatant with lip balm, but it really will work pretty well in emergencies.

Line-cleaner floatant. What if it's really not your day and you've not only lost your floatant, but you don't have any lip balm in your vest either? If you have some line cleaner tucked away in a pocket, you'll still be out of the woods, because most line cleaners are specifically formulated to leave a coating on the fly line to help it float— they'll float your fly, too!

Albolene cream floatant. Speaking of floatants, how would you like to have a lifetime supply for less than $10? Go to the cosmetic department in your local drugstore and pick up a jar of Albolene cream. It is used as a make-up remover and skin conditioner and comes in a one-pound jar. Maybe it's not quite as good as some of the commercial floatants (although it works *better* than some), but it does work great as a floatant, and a pound will last you and your fishing companions a long, long time.

Mud leader-sink treatment. If it's your leader sinking treatment that's missing, you can usually get the leader to sink pretty well if you scoop up a little mud from the streambank and rub the leader down with it. This roughens up the smooth surface a bit and helps it break through the surface tension of the water.

Toothpaste leader-sink treatment. Toothpaste works really well as a leader sink treatment. One of those small tubes that come in travel kits will last you a season or two. It also works pretty well to get the fish smell off of your hands (if you find that offensive).

Cotton-rounds cleaning patches. Cotton rounds (the kind you can buy at the drugstore) make great line-cleaning patches. If you carry a few soaked in liquid soap in one zip-closure plastic bag and some dry ones in another, you can clean your line with the soaped pads, rinse it in the stream, and then dry it with the dry pads. It'll float like new. It'll shoot better, too.

Sand as desiccant. You can come up with a usable desiccant from plain old river sand. Rinse the sand in a tea strainer and save the coarser sand particles in a small container. (Wash the strainer real well before sneaking it back into the kitchen drawer.) Sand isn't quite as effective as the purchased stuff, but it's free. I don't mind paying for the commercial kind, but it's nice to know that if you forget or lose yours, you can get by with what's available along the river.

Fixing loose ferrules with Hard-as-Nails fingernail hardener. You arrive at your destination, hundreds of miles from home, for those long-awaited few days of fishing. As you set up your rod, you notice that the ferrule joint seems loose. Sure enough, when you start casting, the sections keep loosening up after every few casts. Instead of scrapping a day's fishing to drive into the nearest town large enough to have a fly shop, in the vain hope that it can make the repair while you wait, try this trick for a temporary fix.

Get a bottle of Hard-as-Nails fingernail hardener from the local convenience store and brush a couple of coats on the male ferrule; allow it to dry. When it's completely dry (five minutes will usually be long enough), take some emery paper and gently sand down the nail hardener, trying the fit often, until the sections fit together smoothly and tightly.

This isn't a permanent fix, but it will hold up well through at least a half-dozen or so assembly and disassembly operations. It can, of course, be repeated if necessary until you can get the rod in for a permanent repair.

Wiping the rod sections. Graphite rod sections are joined by integral ferrules: the narrow end of one section fits in the wide end of the next. You can eliminate virtually all of the wear at the ferrules by the simple act of wiping off the male section before assembling your rod each time. The fine sand and dirt that the rod picks up when being assembled and disassembled acts as an abrasive between the surfaces as they flex during casting.

Trash-bag wader liners. The bottom end of a trash bag, or even a gallon-size freezer bag, will work to keep your foot dry when you have a leak in the foot section of your wader.

Velcro fastener fly patch. Most fly vests have a lamb's wool patch that you can hook your loose flies in to dry. Mine usually has a couple dozen well-dried flies on it by season's end, because I never get around to putting them back in the fly boxes. If you need a patch but just don't happen to have any lamb's wool around the house, a piece of the looped half of a Velcro fastener will work very well.

Zip-closure bags to store leaders. Some leaders come in nice little zip-closure bags, which work very well, while others come in a package of stiff plastic wrapped around a card, which is almost impossible to reuse. A sandwich-sized plastic zip-closure bag works better than either. It's large enough to get your fingers into and yet will fold up as small as the original packaging.

Extra car keys. It's only happened to me once, but that's enough. Returning to the car wearing the glow from a great afternoon of fishing, I found my car keys were "missing." Well, they were missing from my pocket, but hanging smartly in the ignition, and of course the car was locked. A quarter of an hour's search finally located a piece of loose fence wire that I could fashion into a hook. It only took another 40 minutes or so of contortions and gyrations before I was able to catch the door lock and get in. The glow I wore coming to the car turned into a blue haze surrounding it by the time I got inside. Could've been worse—there was only about 10 minutes of daylight left! Now I carry sets of keys for both cars in a 35-mm film container in my vest.

Sock reel cover. You can buy several styles of covers that will protect your reel while it's on the rod; they do the job very well. An old sock pulled up over the butt of the rod *and* over the reel will do a good job of protecting both, and the price is right, even if you buy a new sock to accent the color of the wraps on your rod.

Insect repellent. Wash your hands thoroughly after applying insect repellent; some repellents will literally melt your fly line, rain jacket, or anything else made of synthetics.

Storing damp rods. The aluminum rod case that comes with most high-quality rods is great for protecting your investment from bumps and bangs, but don't ever put your rod away in it wet. The moisture will be trapped in the case. It can ruin the finish on your rod and corrode some reel seats. It can completely ruin a cane rod.

Ultraviolet rays. Ultraviolet rays from sunlight weaken monofilament pretty rapidly. Don't leave your tippet spools or packages of leaders lying up on the dashboard or on the seat in your vehicle.

Golfer's towel. One of the handiest things to have along on the stream is a small towel. A golfer's towel has a grommet in one corner so it can be attached to a golf cart or bag. The grommet works just as well for attaching it to your vest. It's nice to have a place to dry your fingers while tying on a new dry fly, to avoid wetting it in the process. If you need to handle a fish before releasing it, here's the place to wipe your hands, instead of on your waders. Those of us who wear glasses are always thankful to have a place to wipe them when it starts raining. That net ring just below the back collar on your vest is the ideal place to hang the towel. It's high enough so the towel won't drag in the water, is easily reached, and won't be in your way while fishing.

35-mm film containers. The containers that 35-mm film comes in are among the handiest things you can have with you on a fishing trip. They can serve as auxiliary or emergency fly boxes, as a means of sharing fly floatant or desiccant with your fishing partner (*you'd never forget *yours,* would you?*), as places to keep a spare tip guide and adhesive stick, as containers for captured insects that you want to identify later, and so on, ad infinitum. The only problem is that most of them are black. If you have four or five of them in various vest pockets, you'll have to keep opening them until you find what you're looking for. The obvious solution is to use a color code or in some

way make them distinguishable from one another. There are two easy solutions. (1) Visit your local film-processing center; they usually have the things by the hundreds, and they come in colors other than black (but at a ratio, it seems, of about one to a hundred). They probably will let you dig through the box to find yourself an assortment of colors. (2) Seek out a photographer. Because they're big users of film and know that you don't send the little container in with your film to be developed, they will probably be pleased to be rid of a few. They generally use a variety of brands and types of film, so there may be an assortment of colors there as well.

A trip bag. Did you ever notice how your vest gets heavier and heavier as the season goes along? It's the result of adding one or two little things for this trip, something else for another, and never taking anything out. The best fix for this is to *really* unload your vest. Unload it into a small bag, something along the lines of a carry-on bag, and then always take the bag with you—it's now a trip bag (Fig. 4). Some things will always be in or on your vest, of course: basic fly boxes, leaders and tippet material, clippers, forceps, etc. Spare spools, bulk quantities of flies, extra tippet material, a rain jacket, spare socks, fingerless gloves (mine were still in my vest in August!), a wader repair kit, an extra pair of glasses, zip-closure bags, empty film canisters, plastic bandages, Hard-as-Nails nail hardener, emery paper, and the like can all stay in the trip bag until you get to the stream. Then only put in your vest those things you need for the next few hours of fishing.

The only difficult part is being diligent about unloading your vest at day's end. It's made easier and thus more likely to happen now that you have a specific place for it all, which is there at the same time you're breaking down your rod and putting it and your reel away.

Trip-saver bag. You can make your trip bag into a trip-saver bag with just a little expansion of the contents. Add some tools, especially a set of small screwdrivers and needle-nosed pliers for rod and reel repairs. Some rod winding thread, a couple of sizes of tip guides and an adhesive stick, a spare reel, and first-aid items take up very little room, but can truly salvage a trip that has gone bad.

4. The trip bag.

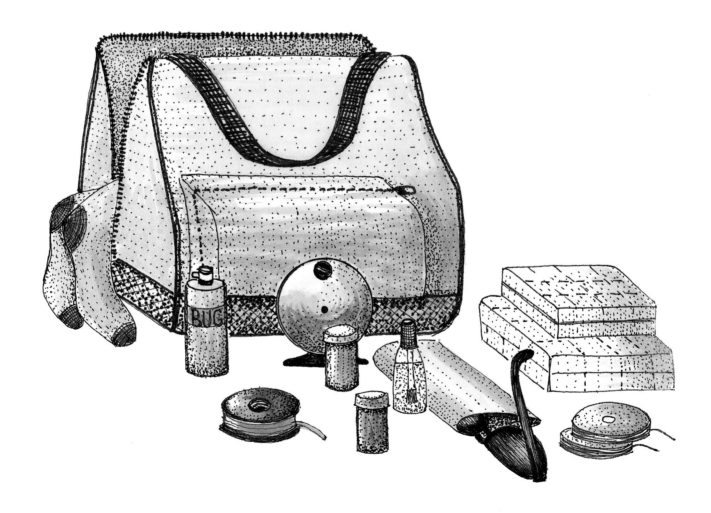

Phil Camera

Finding pinhole leaks in waders.
Pinhole leaks in waders can be very difficult to locate. By inserting a drop light into your waders and turning off all the room lights, you can make the job much easier. The light from the inside will show through the tiniest pinhole, showing you the location of the leak.

Pantyhose seine. An excellent quick and easy insect seine can be fashioned by slipping a section of old pantyhose over your landing net. The nylon mesh is fine enough to trap almost all aquatic insects.

Monofilament sewing thread for tippet. We all know what it's like to reach for your tippet spool, only to find that you're out of 6X or 7X tippet. By keeping a spool of translucent monofilament sewing thread (hemming thread) in your vest, you'll never be without the extra-fine tippet material you need when a midge hatch comes off. It is about 7X (.004 inch diameter), but will cover for 6X in a pinch.

Pipe-insulation helper grip. When you find yourself with an opportunity to fish for large fish and you don't have a rod with a helper grip, you can solve the problem with a 5- or 6-inch (12 or 15 cm) piece of foam pipe insulation from your local hardware store. It comes already slit, so you can fit it over your rod just above the handle, allowing you to grip your rod higher for more comfort during a long-lasting fight.

Homemade stretchable leader. If you are having the problem of breaking off fish because you have a stiff rod or the species you are trying to catch has a very soft mouth, a shock or stretch leader section can save the day. There are commercially made products that you can find in most fly shops, but if you don't have one along, a 10-inch (25 cm) stretchable butt section can be made right at streamside as follows:

1. Cut a piece of heavy leader material approximately 30 inches (76 cm) long.
2. Fold in half and tie a double surgeon's knot on the folded end.
3. Put the loop over something stationary (such as your reel handle), and spiral the loose ends together all the way to the end.
4. Tie a double surgeon's knot to leave a loop of about 3 inches (7.5 cm).

This forms a loop-ended braid section to go between your leader butt and the fly line. If you pull on both ends of the loop, you'll see the amount of stretch you will gain.

Al Diem

Visible drag setting. I want a light, strong reel for trout fishing. When I am after large fish such as salmon and saltwater species, a reel that has a visible drag setting is a great advantage. We sometimes loosen the drag when stringing up our rod or tighten the drag when we've reeled in the line to move to another spot. I've lost fish by forgetting to reset the drag and then hooking up on the first cast with the drag too tight or too loose. If the reel has a visible drag setting, a quick glance will tell you where the drag is set. Most reels don't have such markings, but a few small dabs of paint around the drag knob will serve the same purpose.

Avoid shiny reels. Avoid reels with a bright, shiny finish. As you move the rod during the casting stroke, the sunlight reflecting off the reel will be bouncing all over the place; if it's striking the water, it may spook some fish. They will generally tolerate a steady spot of glare, but the flashing glare will surely put them down.

Long rod. There are several advantages to a longer rod. It allows you to control the line more easily when casting; the extra reach it provides makes it easier to mend the line on the water; and it lets you reach further to dap your fly on the water in places you can't reach with a cast. A longer rod is a real boon when fishing out of a float tube; it gives you more height above the water when casting, and the longer reach allows you more versatility in working the fly in the water.

Polarized sunglasses. You really need to see what's going on when flyfishing, so polarized glasses are an absolute must. It's not unusual to see a flyfisher with a $500 rod, $300 reel, $300 breathable waders, $100 wading shoes, and a $150 vest, but wearing a $5 pair of glasses. Your success will improve greatly with a pair of good-quality polarized glasses.

Jerry Gibbs

Straightening monofilament. Forget the old piece of rubber you used to rub on monofilament leaders to straighten them; use your thumb instead. Friction/heat is what causes the monofilament to straighten, but it also can cause a loss of strength. Rubbing a leader over rubber causes more weakening than rubbing it over your thumb, because you can control the heat buildup by feel on your thumb, although today's super mono leaders can take a bit more heat than the older formulations.

Super lines. Because of their small diameter for strength, the braided, so-called super lines made of polyethylene allow you to spool more backing on a reel, thus turning a very small reel into one you can use when larger fish are expected. There are a couple of cautionary notes when using them, though. Wind the polyethylene stuff onto the reel with quick back-and-forth movements to keep the fine-diameter braid from cutting down into the remaining backing. Also, watch your fingers; the material can cut like a razor.

Squashing hook barbs. Most anglers pinch down the barbs on their hooks with pliers crossways to the barb. It works some of the time, but it can also break off the hoop point—disastrous if you've found the "right" fly and have only one. Instead, keep your pliers parallel to the hook point and barb when squashing.

Stringing your rod. When stringing up your fly rod, don't pull the line/leader from the tip guide so that the upper rod section takes a severe bend. Let the handle sit on a hard surface (the ground is fine) and grasp the rod higher up, so when you pull out line, the rod tip section is not elbowed over. Despite vast improvements in today's graphite rods, putting an acute bend in the tip is still an easy way to snap it.

Beads. You don't need to be a fly-tyer to give a nymph or streamer a bit of extra enticement. Slip one or two tiny glass or bright metal beads on the tippet before tying on your fly. Then pin the beads against the hook eye by tying a nail knot around the tippet with a piece of monofilament, or by adding a small float stop. In addition to gaining a bit of flash and color, the fly will sink a bit faster.

Check ferrules. When fishing with multipiece rods (especially older models), periodically check the ferrules. The more ferrules, the better the odds for a section to loosen. Casting with a slightly separated section can cause rod breakage.

Tape. Always bring a roll of silver duct tape and a roll of black electrician's tape on fishing trips. You'll use them in undreamed-of ways. Use them over the zippers of your duffel bags or to patch a hundred and one things. I once saved a day's fishing by taping over a hole in a boat's fuel hose.

Joan Wulff

Third-generation graphite rods. Third-generation graphite benefits all anglers, but is particularly exciting for women. Lighter than other graphites, the rods also have exceptional quickness, sending the fly to its target with almost no undulation or wavering, as has been so common in the past.

Rod length for short people. A misconception that works against women in flyfishing is that short people should use short fly rods. It's really just the opposite. What the rod lacks in length, the caster has to make up for with longer strokes. Stroke length is limited by arm length. Short people have short arms. Logic class—the shorter you are, the more a longer rod will do for you.

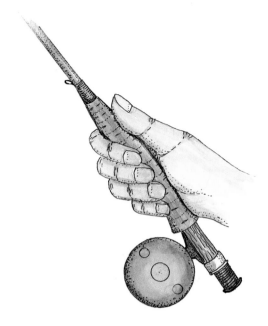

Grip size and shape. When flycasting, your hand is working constantly, so if the diameter of the grip is too large or swells in the wrong place, you'll suffer for it. When you are choosing your fly rod, check the different shapes of grips available; if you cannot get what you want, sandpaper may solve the problem. Cork can be sanded away to give you a more comfortable fit.

Tippet length and diameter. When adding tippet to step down in size, taper it with 8- to 12-inch-long pieces. Drop down **in diameter** .002 inch—or two X-designations—at a time, until you reach the **final tippet section** next to the fly.

Make that final piece of tippet longer. As you go down in strength, go up in length. A characteristic of monofilament is that it stretches. With a short leader tippet of fine diameter, the shock of a trout's jumps and surges is much more likely to use up that stretch and break it than would happen with a longer tippet. The additional stretch acts as a cushion for those shocks.

Strength of a tippet. At the beginning of every season, or at least once in your life, you should make up a leader with 3 feet of 5X for the tippet. Tie the tippet end around a post, the bumper of your car, or some other stationary object. Put a bend in your rod as if you had a fish hooked, and see if you can break the tippet with this bent-rod pull. Do not exceed the 90-degree playing angle with the rod.

It is incredible to realize the strength of so light a tippet. It is about 4-pound test, and I doubt you can break it. Even a 7X tippet can be 2-pound test. It will open your eyes, and you'll know something 99 out of 100 fishermen don't: how much pressure the tippet can stand on a straight, hard pull. Try more than one strength of tippet, so you can compare them. This

is the strength you'll call on when playing a fish under the condition of static pressure.

Vests for women. Most vests are marketed for men, with the focus on the number of pockets they contain. With their broad backs and large chests, men have plenty of body room for an array of chock-full pockets. Not so for women. We need fewer pockets and must fill them carefully so our breasts will not be uncomfortable from bulk or jabbed by sharp edges.

Keep all the bulky boxes and items in the outside pockets, and use the inside pockets for leaders and tippet spools, licenses, and other flat things. Another area to think about is between your armpit and waist. A filled pocket near the side seams should not force your upper arm away from your body, either while casting or while fishing the fly.

Because women vary so much in neck-to-waist length and bosom size, I can't give a blanket description of which vest will suit you. Choose carefully, that's all. Large-chested women have the hardest time finding something perfect and often must buy a man's vest.

chapter two

Fly Selection

The Basics

Trout feed primarily on aquatic insects; the most common of these belong to four large biological categories called orders. The mayflies (order Ephemeroptera) and caddisflies (order Trichoptera) are the most prevalent; consequently, imitations of those are the flies used most often by the flyfisher. The stoneflies (order Plecoptera) and the midges (order Diptera) have their periods of dominance in many trout streams, so flies are tied to imitate them also.

You don't need a degree in aquatic entomology to be an effective flyfisher, but there is some basic knowledge that you need for better understanding of what's going on in the stream. You'll be able to communicate more effectively with other anglers and better understand the literature of the sport if your knowledge base includes some familiarity with the insects found in trout streams. Let's take a quick look at these four orders of insects and their life cycles.

Mayflies (order Ephemeroptera)

The mayflies undergo incomplete metamorphosis. Their life cycle is composed of egg, nymph, and adult. They are unique among the aquatic insects in that they have two stages as an adult: dun (subimago) and spinner (imago).

Insect eggs are microscopic; therefore, we don't try to imitate that stage of any of the insects. Mayfly nymphs range in size from less than an eighth of an inch (.3 cm) to nearly an inch long (2.5 cm; see Fig. 1). Their colors vary from grey, to brown, to olive, but the colors are generally mottled and subdued. They have two or three tails, a segmented abdomen, and an enlarged thorax with a wingcase on top. The nymphs live in the stream for one to three years; thus, even though they're not just swimming around freely as food for the trout, there is plenty of opportunity for them to get washed out from under the rocks and vegetation they inhabit and become a trout snack. Their sheer numbers and the length of time that they are in the stream make them important in the diet of the trout.

The mature mayfly nymph swims to the surface, the wingcase splits open, and the adult (we anglers call it a dun, while the entomologist refers to it as a subimago) crawls out through the opening. We sometimes use emerger patterns (often, nymphs fished just under the surface) or wet flies to imitate this very active pre-hatch activity of the nymph (Fig. 2).

While it is emerging, and for a period of a few seconds to a couple of minutes after, the dun floats along on the surface of the stream and is quite vulnerable to the trout. This is what we are trying to duplicate with a dry-fly imitation of the mayfly.

The mayfly dun ranges in color from pale cream, through yellow, to reddish brown. It also occurs in all shades of grey and brown, as well as shades of olive, depending on species. The distinctive characteristic of the adult mayfly is that it carries its wings upright.

The surviving duns molt again (generally in nearby brush) into the sexually mature stage: the spinner or imago (Fig. 3). Spinners are typically larger and more brightly colored than duns, and their wings become clear. The mature insects then mate (typically in flight, over the water), and the female deposits the eggs in the stream to begin the cycle anew. The mayflies can't feed or take on water, so they die very quickly—many species die the same day that they hatch.

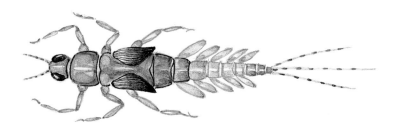

1. The mayfly nymph.

2. The mayfly dun.

3. The mayfly spinner.

Caddisflies (order Trichoptera)

Caddisflies develop through complete metamorphosis: egg, larva, pupa, and adult. There is no nymphal stage, but the imitations of the larval and pupal stages are called nymphs, and the method of fishing those imitations is considered nymphing. The flyfisher seeks to imitate all of the stages except the egg.

Caddis larvae are wormlike creatures. There are a few species that are free-living; they attach themselves to rocks or vegetation with a strand of silk and range about somewhat, feeding on microscopic food particles. Most species, however, build an open-ended case of sand particles or vegetation around themselves, which is firmly attached to something in the stream. They are less available to the trout than the free-living species, but the trout will root them from their attachment and eat case and all.

The free-living species vary in coloration, including olive, grey, tan to brown, and cream (Fig. 4). The color of the case of the case-building species is dependent, of course, on the construction material (Fig. 5). Common larva and pupa sizes are from 1/16 to 3/4 inch long (.15 to 2 cm).

As they approach maturity, the free-living species spin a sealed cocoon, while the case-builders seal up their case, except for a tiny opening; both then enter a period of pupation (Fig. 6). When fully mature, they exit their case or cocoon and move to the surface to hatch into their adult forms (Fig. 7).

Unlike the mayflies, most caddis species hatch very quickly after reaching the surface of the stream and immediately fly off into the surrounding brush to mate. The adult insect is very mothlike in silhouette; its wings are carried in an inverted *V* shape over its back.

After mating, the female returns to the stream to lay her eggs. Some species swim back down into the stream, some crawl down rocks or other structures, and still others fly along with their abdomens trailing in the water to wash off the eggs. Adult caddisflies are found in the same colors as the larvae and the pupae, usually subdued colors.

Stoneflies (order Plecoptera)

Like mayflies, stoneflies undergo incomplete metamorphosis, so there is a nymphal stage (Fig. 8).

The stonefly nymph looks a lot like the mayfly nymph, but is usually more robust and has two wingcases. Many of the species are grey, brownish, or olive, but there are several that show amber coloration, and a few even display some orange or red.

Stonefly nymphs are rather active in the stream as they forage for food; hence they probably become available to the trout more frequently than mayfly nymphs or caddis larvae. That's not to say that they make up a majority of the trout's food, though. In most

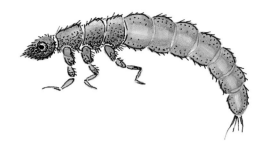

4. Free-living caddis larva.

5. Cased caddis larva.

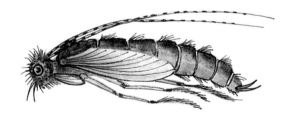

6. The caddis pupa.

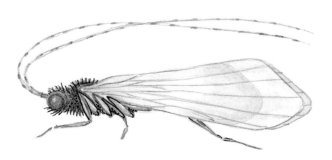

7. The adult caddisfly.

streams the numbers of caddis and mayflies are considerably greater than the stonefly population. Although they are not quite as available, caddisflies and mayflies make up a greater portion of the trout's food. Even though they may not be available in great numbers, stonefly nymphs are frequently available, and the trout seem to expect them about anytime.

Stonefly nymphs don't come to the water's surface to hatch. They crawl out of the stream on rocks or vegetation; the adults emerge there, out of the water.

After mating, the females return to the stream to lay their eggs. Some become available to the trout at that time. Stoneflies are clumsy fliers, which probably accounts for some ending up in the water as food for the trout. Stonefly adults (Fig. 9) carry their wings folded flat over their back; in silhouette, they look a lot like caddisfly adults.

Midges (order Diptera)

Midges are probably the least important kinds of insects for most flyfishers. Midges develop through complete

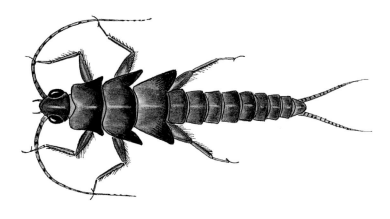

8. The stonefly nymph.

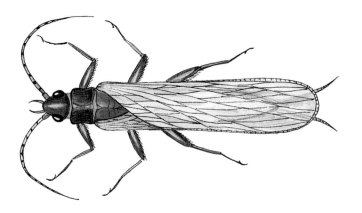

9. The adult stonefly.

10. The midge larva.

11. The midge pupa.

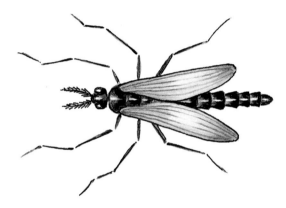

12. The adult midge.

metamorphosis. They don't have a nymphal stage, even though we call the imitations of the larva and pupa "nymphs." As the common name suggests, most midges are small, and some are downright minuscule.

Midge larvae and pupae generally look like tiny little worms (Figs. 10 and 11). They show the whole range of colors found in the other insects we've discussed. Dark grey and brown shades are the most common.

The adult midge carries its two wings in a flat *V* shape, like a common housefly (Fig. 12). Because the insects are so small and their wings are clear, the wings are often left off imitations.

Although adult midges are not prevalent enough on many streams to attract much attention from either the trout or the flyfisher, there are exceptions. On our home stream, we get some really great dry-fly fishing on bright, sunny days in February and March. A 12- or 14-inch (30 or 35 cm) trout on a 7X tippet and a #24 fly will warm you up...even in February in Colorado.

Other Flies

In addition to the flies that are tied to imitate aquatic insects, the flyfisher uses patterns that are meant to simulate terrestrial insects such as grasshoppers, crickets, ants, beetles, and bees (Fig. 13).

There are also a group of fly patterns called attractors. These are flies that aren't tied to represent any particular insect. Humpies and the Wulff series are examples of very effective attractors. Their success probably lies in the fact that they look kind of generically "buggy." Even though they don't imitate anything specific, they look a lot like many insects. The attractor patterns are often the first choice of the experienced flyfisher when there isn't a particular insect prevalent on the water (Fig. 14).

Streamers are flies tied to represent minnows or the small fry of game fish. They are tied to be relatively long and slim, dark on top and light-colored on the bottom. Usually, they are tied with metallic material of some kind on the hook shank, so it will flash when moved through the water (Fig. 15).

13. A grasshopper imitation.

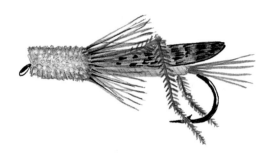

14. An attractor fly.

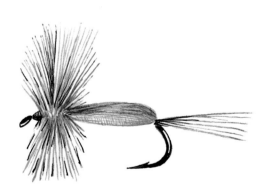

15. A streamer fly.

Basic Selections of the Experts

Most flyfishers have a few select patterns that are always in their fly boxes. The selection may be well thought out, based on known trout preferences on the streams usually fished, or may be simply an assortment of types, colors, and sizes of flies that they think will serve to meet most situations. No two anglers are likely to have the same idea as to the best fly selection.

We thought it would be interesting to find what kind of variety we'd see from among our expert contributors. We asked each of our contributing experts to choose three patterns of each type (dry flies, wet flies, nymphs, and streamers) that they would choose to have in their fly boxes if they were restricted to that selection for all of their trout fishing. Here are their choices.

Phil Camera

Dry flies: Parachute Adams, Elk-Hair Caddis, Griffith Gnat
Wet flies/emergers: LaFontaine Sparkle Caddis, Heathen, Soft Hackle Emerger
Nymphs: Gold-Ribbed Hare's Ear, Pheasant Tail, Prince Nymph
Streamers: Wooly Bugger, Bunny Leach, Muddler Minnow

Al Diem

Dry flies: Muddler (fished dry), Gray Wulff, Elk-Hair Caddis

Wet flies/emergers: Muddler (wet), Gold-Ribbed Hare's Ear, Damsel Fly Emerger
Nymphs: Bead-Head Pheasant Tail, Stonefly Nymph, Small Wooly Bugger
Streamers: Silver Muddler, Herbie Johnson Streamer (salmon fly), Wooly Bugger

Paul Fling

Dry flies: Foam-Body Caddis, Royal Wulff, Poly-Wing Dry-Fly
Wet flies/emergers: Caddis Emerger, LaFontaine Sparkle Pupa, Pheasant-Tail Emerger
Nymphs: Gold-Ribbed Hare's Ear, Bead-Head Pheasant Tail, Rubberband Stonefly
Streamers: Muddler Minnow, Wooly Bugger, Matuka

Jerry Gibbs

Dry flies: Adams, Light Cahill, Royal Wulff, Griffith's Gnat
Wet flies/emergers: Gold-Ribbed Hare's Ear, Royal Coachman, Emerging Caddis
Nymphs: Gold-Ribbed Hare's Ear, Prince Nymph, Stonefly Nymph
Streamers: Muddler Minnow, Wooly Bugger, Bunny Fly

Don Puterbaugh

Dry flies: Foam-Body Caddis, Blue-Winged Olive, Yellow-Foam Stonefly

Wet flies/emergers: Caddis Emerger, Mini-Muddler, Pale Morning Dun Emerger

Nymphs: Golden Stonefly, Pheasant Tail, Bead-Head Brassie

Streamers: Marabou Black-Nosed Dace, Mini-Muddler, Wooly Bugger

Joan Wulff

Dry flies: Royal Wulff, Adams, Blue-Winged Olive

Wet flies/emergers: Hare's Ear, Soft Hackle, Midge Pupa

Nymphs: Brown Stonefly, Pheasant Tail, Bead-Head

Streamers: Muddler Minnow, Surface Stone (fished wet), Wooly Bugger

Keep in mind that all of these choices are made blind: these are the selections each expert has made without knowing any specifics about where or when he or she will be fishing.

Fly Selection Tips and Techniques

Here are some tips and techniques to help you with fly selection when you are fishing a specific stream.

Getting fly information. The easiest way to get an idea of what fly to use is to visit the local fly shop. The people

there meet a lot of anglers and also probably have some guides on the river, so they're pretty sure to know what's going on. If you're going some distance to fish, don't hesitate to give one of the fly shops in the area you'll be visiting a call; they'll be glad to provide you with the most current information that they have. There are a number of books available that include hatching charts, which show the hatches on major streams at different times of the year. They can help you decide on what to take along if you can't find a way to make direct contact.

Scouting. Even given the most current information, it's usually up to you to find out specifically what's happening on the section of the stream that you're fishing. Most of us would save a lot of fishing time by doing some scouting *before* tying on our fly and heading down to the river. Usually, however, we tie on the pattern we want to use at the car, go to the river, and spend some time finding out that it was the wrong choice before we settle down and take the time to read the signs that are there.

Spider webs. If there are rising trout, it's not too difficult to find out what they are feeding on. Small insects on

16. Spider webs often
hold samples of active
insects.

the water are hard to see, though. A squatting stance with your eye close to the water surface will help. Look in the back eddies behind rocks and obstructions where the insects tend to collect. There are always some spider webs in the rock crevices and branches along the stream and if the hatch is, or has been, significant there will probably be a few samples collected there (Fig. 16).

Maybe there is evidence in the back eddies and spider webs that a hatch has been occurring, but there's no sign of rising trout. In that case, you'll probably need to go to an underwater imitation of that insect in the form of a wet fly or nymph.

Birds. Keep an eye on the area above the water, too. Birds gathering above the stream and dipping down to the surface and back up into the air often are the first sign that a hatch is starting to come off, or that it's about time for it to come off. That's usually a pretty

17. A gathering of birds over the water may announce a hatch.

good hint that it's time to change to a dry fly to match the insects you've seen or have reason to expect (Fig. 17).

Time of day and weather affect a hatch. A couple of other keys that might help you have a better idea of what to expect are the time of day and the weather. Some species, such as the pale morning duns, are morning and late evening hatching mayflies. Others, such as the blue-winged olives, usually hatch in subdued light during midday, so if the fellow at the fly shop told you there was a good hatch of pale morning duns coming off the river each day, you wouldn't

expect to see them at midday. There are always exceptions, though. An overcast day will often see the hatch extended pretty much throughout the day, although heavier in the morning and in the evening.

When you find some blue-winged olives caught in the spider webs along the stream, you'd expect them to begin hatching around midday. A cloudy, warm morning, however, may bring the hatch on earlier, maybe mid-morning. There are no definitive rules here; just be sensitive to any known facts about the insects and then look for outside influences that might modify their expected behavior.

In a few cases, the response of the insects to weather phenomena is striking. We were fishing in Wyoming one year in the spring and the blue-winged olives were prevalent, but only when it was cloudy—to the extent that we could predict trout activity by watching the sky for passing clouds. I spent one afternoon sitting at a picnic table by the water reading a book and only getting into the water when I would see a cloud headed in our direction. You could actually see the trout rising only within the cloud's shadow as it passed down-stream. We've not seen such a prevalent response since, but we do know that blue-winged olives hatch in greatly increased numbers on cloudy days; that information allows us to be ready for that particular hatch on those days.

Before the hatch. While you're waiting for the hatch to begin, you should be catching some fish on an imitation of the underwater stage of the insect, either a nymph or a wet-fly/emerger pattern. There are a couple of ways to figure out what pattern type to use.

If you have a basic understanding of the insects trout feed on, you know what the nymphal and emerging stages of the insect look like, because you know whether it's a mayfly, stonefly, caddisfly, or midge. Determining the size is easily done by looking at the size of the adults you found; nymphs are usually about one size smaller. Color choice is a bit more difficult, because the adult coloration is often different than the underwater stage.

The underwater stages of most insects, though, are pretty drab—olive, grey, brown, or, most often, a mix of those colors—and most nymph patterns use those colors. If you have any nymphs at all in your fly box, you probably have something of the right color.

Inspect the site. A visual inspection is the most reliable source of information. Gently lift some rocks from the stream bed, turn them over, and see what kind of critters are hiding there. The most prevalent insects may not be what's the most available to the trout as food and may not be the insect that will make up the hatch, but, lacking any other data to go on, it's not a bad place to start in making your choice of a pattern with which to begin fishing.

Seining for insects. Another method for finding out what insects are active and most available to the trout is to do a little seining. There are several types of insect seines on the market for just this purpose, but a piece of cheese-cloth mounted on a couple of small sticks works fine. It can be improved on by using a piece of pantyhose or nylon stocking instead of cheesecloth. Aquarium nets work fine, although they're a bit small. All you're after is a fabric that will let the water flow through while catching the insect. The nets work equally well for capturing adult insects from the surface or nymphs and emergers from beneath the surface.

Unless there's a lot of insect activity, you're not going to find great numbers of insects in your net, but you only need one or two to see what they look like so you can match them. Adults are relatively easy to catch, because you can see them floating on the surface, although you may have to be patient until one comes within arm's reach.

Patience is really the secret to success in capturing some samples from underwater. Submerge the net just below the surface and hold it there for a couple of minutes, and then check to see what you've caught. If that's not successful after a couple of tries, lower the net to a different depth. If there's any specific insect activity worth noting, you'll find evidence in your net.

Making a dry fly into a nymph.
Occasions will arise when you think you've figured out what the trout are feeding on but you don't have a fly with you to duplicate the stage of the insect that you want to imitate. Take heart; you may be able to make do with something else in your fly box.

You can convert a dry fly of the right color and size into a passable nymph by trimming off the wings and all of the hackle except for a few barbules left on the bottom side to imitate legs. You may need to trim those a little shorter to get the right appearance. You can trim the wing shorter, instead of removing it completely, and cut off most of the hackle for a wet-fly or emerger imitation (Fig. 18).

You can fish a nymph or a cut-down dry fly as an emerger by treating your leader with floatant so that the fly drifts on, or just under, the surface. Swisher and Richards, in their book *Fly Fishing Strategies* (Crown, 1975), report unusually good success during hatches when they imitated stillborn mayflies. You may be able to use a nymph or wet-fly imitation floating in the surface film when you don't have a good dry-fly imitation to match hatching insects. The whole point of this is to show that you can be innovative and often make do with something other than the "just right" imitation for a given situation.

If you're a fly-tyer, you have the additional option of going back to the car and tying up a few of whatever pattern you need—assuming, of course that you have your flytying kit along in your trip-saver bag. The negative side of this solution is that you're using up valuable fishing time. By the time you can get to the car, whip up a few flies, and get back to the stream, the nymphs or emergers may be hatching as adults or, if it's the adults that you're tying to imitate, the hatch may be over.

Finding what insects the trout are feeding on, or are most likely to feed on, is a very important step in the fly selection process, but there are times when using the best imitation may not be practical.

Pocket-water flies. You're standing at the bottom of a 200-foot (61 m) run of river tumbling its way through a maze of rocks and boulders. There are dozens of little slicks and tiny pools of calmer water in front and behind the rocks that are sure to hold fish, because the fish can sit in the quieter

water and have a lot of food presented to them by the fast water. This is classic pocket-water fishing, which is overlooked by the majority of flyfishers.

It may well be that there's a hatch of small caddisflies coming off for which a #18 Elk-Hair Caddis is a perfect match, but it's not going to work very well here. You're going to be making rather short casts to the very small targets presented by those tiny little slick runs. The fly will only be on the water for a second or two before it's swept downstream in the rush of fast water. You're not going to be able to see that little #18 amidst the visual chaos. Although the trout is in a great spot to have a lot of food go by, it's at

18. *Converting a dry fly to a nymph.*

a disadvantage in that the food is going by very quickly, with no chance for a long searching look to be sure it's appearance is just right.

Tie on a #14 Elk-Hair Caddis of the color to match the naturals that are hatching, and have at it. You've matched the color and silhouette that the trout is looking for and, although you may, in fact, get fewer takes than if you were presenting a #18, you'll be able to see the takes and you'll actually *catch* a lot more fish.

Blotting your fly. When fishing pocket water, your fly is going to get drowned at the end of each drift, and you'll have to be a little more diligent about keeping it floating. You'll be doing a lot of false-casting when fishing this pocket water in order to judge constantly changing casting distances; that false-casting will help to dry your fly between drifts. You can help the process greatly by blotting the water out of the fly after every few casts. Press it against your vest or shirt sleeve; you're just trying to get the majority of the water off the fly so that your false casts can dry it better. This won't completely negate the need to stop casting, put the fly in your desiccant, and re-treat it with floatant, but it will keep the fly floating for more casts between those stops. We've never caught a trout on a fly in the desiccant container.

Weighting methods. When you're fishing nymphs, wet flies, or streamers, you have a choice of three methods to get your fly down into the lower reaches of a stream: use a weighted fly, weight the leader, or do both. Doing both is only called for when you need to get really deep and you're fishing fast water. Casting a weighted fly or a weighted leader is more difficult and less pleasurable than casting un-weighted by a long shot. Casting a weighted fly *and* leader is just plain horrible—about as much fun as shutting the car door on your rod, but it lasts longer!

In the fall, we do a lot of nymphing using small #18 and #20 flies; the amount of weight that it is practical to apply to the hook is tiny. Casting these weighted flies is very little different from casting unweighted; since the fly is so small, not much weight is needed to get it to sink. Weighting the fly is a good method in this case.

During runoff, when the river is high and fast, we do most of our nymphing with flies in the #12 to #16 range; the hooks are large enough to get a lot of lead on, but they are not much fun to cast. For this fishing we generally use unweighted nymphs and weight the leader with strip-lead, moldable weight, or split shot. Split shot works fine if you only need to put one on your leader. Limit it to just one, because there's little more you can do to insure a tangled leader mess than to string a series of lead balls on it. A continuous strip of lead wound on the leader (Twist-ons or LED) is much less troublesome (Fig. 19).

Weighted flies work fine in small sizes, but, in our opinion, a large weighted fly can't move as freely in the underwater currents as an unweighted version; therefore, it looks less like a natural. Consequently, we prefer to weight the leader instead of the fly when fishing larger nymphs and wet flies, so that the subtle undulations of a natural insect are duplicated by our

fly as it drifts. Streamers also seem to be more effective when the weight is on the leader a foot or so (30 cm) above the fly, so the fly can swing more freely in the water.

A dry-fly indicator. Our home stream, Colorado's Arkansas River, rarely freezes up in the winter, and there are many bright, sunny days when a hatch comes off. The insects that make up the hatch are typically very small; we have to use #22 and #24 flies to get any attention from the feeding trout.

19. Weighting methods

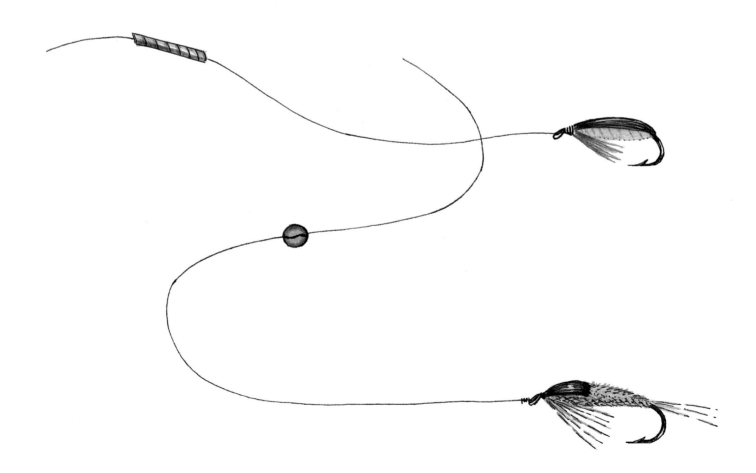

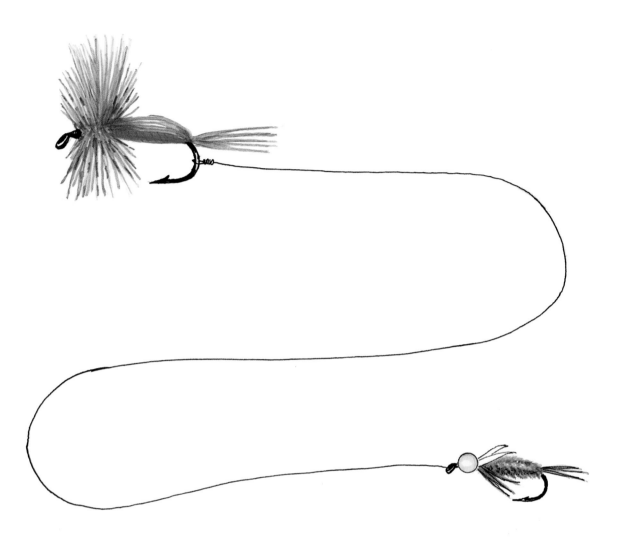

*20. Rigging a dry-fly
indicator.*

It's been a few years since either of us could see a #24 dry fly from 30 feet away, but I'm not about to give up taking these ice-water browns on small dries and fine tippets.

Our solution is simple. We tie a large, easily seen dry fly on the end of the leader and then tie a 3- to 5-foot (1 to 1.5 m) length of tippet to the bend of the large dry; then we put the small dry fly on the end of the tippet section (Fig. 20). Now we have a

strike indicator that we can see during the drift; if there is a rise anywhere near the large fly, it's probably to our small imitation. Since there is an easily seen marker near our small fly, we can often get a visual fix on the small fly and actually follow its drift. By keeping the section between the two flies relatively short (5 feet, or 1.5 m, is about maximum), we rarely have a problem with the two flies tangling.

Fluorescent calf-tail dry flies. Tie up a few large dry flies using fluorescent calf tail for the wing, to use as your indicator flies. It really makes the flies easy to spot. We've had a lot of (dumb?) trout take these large fluorescent-winged creations, so adding the fluorescent material doesn't completely keep the large indicator fly from working. Hot pink seems to be the best color for the wing in most lighting conditions. Chartreuse is also a good choice, but is not quite as visible in flat light conditions.

Alternate rigging for multiple flies. Another technique that we've used is an offshoot of one suggested by Gary LaFontaine (*Challenge of the Trout,* Mountain Press, 1976) for fishing multiple wet flies. When tying your tippet to the leader, leave the tag end (the end you'd normally trim off after the knot is tied) 2 or 3 feet long (.6 m to 1 m), and tie your large dry fly to that. This works pretty well, but it seems that we do get a few more cases of the two leaders tangling using this method. Gary was only using a dropper of 6 inches or so (15 cm) for fishing wet flies.

Short-cast to image the fly. There are times when it's difficult to see your dry fly on the water, either because the sun is creating a lot of glare on the water or a leaden sky is flattening the light so there's no contrast between your fly and the water. In some light, your fly will show up as a bright spot on the water; in other light, it may appear darker than the surface. Until you see it a time or two, you don't really know what you're looking for. A technique that will often help is to make a very short cast—something close enough that you can see your fly—and watch the drift. By doing this, you establish a mental image of what you're looking for on the water. You'll find that spotting and following your fly will be much easier when you extend your cast to fishing distance.

Offsetting small hooks. Really small flies (#18 and smaller) have a very small gap; consequently it's difficult to consistently hook the trout. We've found that we can at least double the hookup rate by simply offsetting the point of the hook so that it's not aligned directly under the hook shank. To offset the point, hold the fly by the

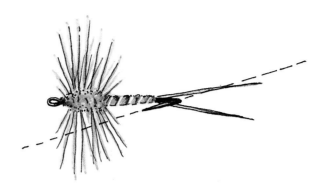

21. Offsetting the point to increase the gap of a small hook.

shank and use your thumb to *gently* bend the point slightly out of alignment (Fig. 21).

Exceptions to the Rule of Four. As we said in Chapter One, the basic rule for selecting the size of your tippet is to divide the size of the fly by four—for example, a 4X tippet for a #16 fly. The rule is based on the stiffness of the tippet necessary to turn a dry fly over at the end of the cast. The bigger the fly, the more force is needed to turn it over. The Rule of Four works very well in most situations. There are times, however, when an exception is appropriate.

When you are casting in the wind, it's advantageous to have a slightly heavier tippet section to overcome the effect of the wind on the cast. Not only will the heavier tippet turn the fly over better, but you can cast more accurately, because the wind will have less effect on the fly's direction as the leader unrolls. If you're using a bushy, wind-resistant fly, it will have the same effect as casting into the wind; again, a

heavier tippet will turn the fly over with greater authority and accuracy.

Casting a dry fly into a dead calm pool where there's not a ripple on the water may require you to go to a lighter tippet. Your leader and tippet will create more commotion on the water surface and will be seen much more easily under these conditions. A lighter tippet will often make the difference between taking some trout and going home skunked. No matter how delicately you cast, the fly line will make some disturbance when it lands on still water. Therefore, it's usually necessary to lengthen your leader so that it presents the fly at a greater distance from the end of the fly line, in addition to going to a lighter tippet when fishing smooth water.

Turning the fly over isn't quite as important when fishing underwater imitations as when you're fishing dry flies, because the current will straighten everything out as the fly sinks. Using a lighter tippet than that which the Rule of Four would call for when fishing nymphs and wet flies will almost always improve your results. We don't think it's so much that the trout can see the heavier tippet and can't see the lighter one. Our feeling is that the lighter tippet allows the fly to drift in a much more natural manner, following all of the side-to-side and up-and-down subtleties of the underwater currents.

Phil Camera

Identify the food source. When selecting a fly to simulate a natural food source, you must first identify the food source you want to simulate. The proper fly will meet these criteria: it must be of the right size, shape, and color. Remember, even if you've picked the right fly for the job, your success will be limited according to the presentation.

Al Diem

Color of flies and water color. When faced with a situation where I'm not sure what color streamer to use, I often fall back to a rather simple formula given me by an Atlantic salmon guide many years ago. Although his approach was meant to be specific to salmon, I've found that it usually works on trout water also. If the water has a reddish color to it (usually from flowing through a peat bog), use black flies with silver tinsel or bead-head. Blue/green water color calls for yellow and/or green flies with gold tinsel or bead-head. Yellow-tinted water should be fished with light-colored flies with silver tinsel or bead-head. I've no idea why the formula works, but it really does in a surprising number of situations.

Water and fly size. A general rule for salmon fishing is that the lower the water, the smaller the fly; I use them as small as #12s. If that doesn't pique the salmon's interest, though, I go to the other extreme with something like a big #2, and that will often result in a strike.

Stonefly imitations. I think stonefly imitations are underused by most anglers as searching patterns. They're especially effective when fishing pocket water and shallow runs. They float well, imitate a food form that is often present, and are large enough to get the trout's attention.

Jerry Gibbs

Bass bugs. Ever think about using bass bugs for trout? For big browns—especially at night—they can be dynamite. The best choice is foam bugs that land with a tiny "splat," which can be burbled and jerked before you cause them to dive beneath the surface. Try them during the day by working them down a run with a little action imparted.

22. A streamside color change with a felt-tip marking pen.

Contrasting flies. When there's no hatch and you want to prospect the water, consider the background against which your attractor fly will be seen, and choose something that contrasts. Metallic flash works, of course, but trout respond well to blue, purple, orange, yellow, red, and chartreuse as well. Choose the hotter colors in the fall, and if all else fails, try black.

Joan Wulff

A streamside color change. You can change the character of a fly by trimming off the wings, the above-water hackles, or everything but the body (to make a pupa). It's hard to make a dark fly light, but with a dark waterproof felt-tip marking pen, you could certainly make a light fly dark (Fig. 22).

chapter three

Reading the Water

The Basics

Flyfishing is a very complex pursuit. It's impossible to categorize the skills needed into a hierarchy by importance. Successful flyfishers need some knowledge of limnology (the study of rivers, lakes, and streams); aquatic entomology (the study of waterborne insects); and trout biology. Flyfishers have to know how to tie some knots, cast well under variable conditions, be able to wade safely and quietly, and they have to be able to read the water. Reading water isn't necessarily more important than the other needed skills, but it is crucial to success.

Trout must have cover from predators, a reliable source of food, and water that they can hold in with the minimal expenditure of energy to survive. Consequently, they hold in greater numbers in certain areas of their environment where the conditions fulfill these requirements. Reading the water is the ability to perceive where the trout are most likely to be and the ability to determine where and how to cast so that your fly is presented to them in the most natural manner.

The places where trout spend most of their time can be divided into the categories of primary lies, feeding lies, and resting lies.

Primary Lies

Primary lies are those where the fish can hold in a quiet current. There they are fully protected from overhead

1. A primary lie.

predators such as fish-eating birds and mammals and are continually present-ed with a large quantity of food (Fig. 1). There aren't many places in a given section of stream that offer all of these amenities, but you can bet that those few places hold the largest trout in the area, because the larger trout take them over and keep the smallfry away.

The most common primary lies are probably undercut banks. Undercut banks occur where the water flow runs into the bank at a sharp angle and washes away the underside of the bank. The outside of a bend is where the deepest undercuts are formed. These undercuts provide the trout with complete overhead protection, the water back under the bank is out of the heavier mainstream flow, and the stream currents carry large quanti-ties of food through the area—break-fast in bed.

Other primary lies can be found in quiet water under overhanging brush, under bridges, and beneath logs that are partially submerged. Anywhere the conditions of overhead protection, quiet water, and a concentration of food are present constitutes a potential primary lie. Look for them and never, ever pass one by, because they almost always hold a nice fish.

The reason for the "almost always" qualifier is that sometimes the trout moves out of its seemingly ideal lie. If, for instance, there is a major hatch or nymphal drift, there are probably some feeding lies that provide more food than the primary lie, and the trout will move

on to a feeding station, even though it temporarily offers less protection.

Feeding Lies

A feeding lie is a position in the stream where food is funneled into a relatively small area. The best feeding lies are adjacent to quiet water, where the trout can hold with little expendi-ture of energy and still be able to reach the food with minimal effort. The quantity of food available normal-ly isn't sufficient to draw trout out of their resting or primary lies into these less-protected areas. When there's a hatch on, or a nymphal drift occur-ring, though, there will be a lot of trout in these locations, and they'll be feeding readily (Fig. 2).

Resting Lies

Resting lies are those locations where trout that aren't big enough to force their way into a primary lie spend their time. Resting lies provide cover (although not always complete over-head coverage) and are in quiet water. Fish lying in a resting lie aren't provided with a lot of food, but will usually take anything that happens within reach. In sections of a stream that offer little in the way of overhead protection, fish will often use water depth to provide the needed cover from predators, and rest near the bottom of the stream (Fig. 3).

Soft Water

When we speak of soft water, we're talking about a stretch of water whose surface is generally smooth—the pools

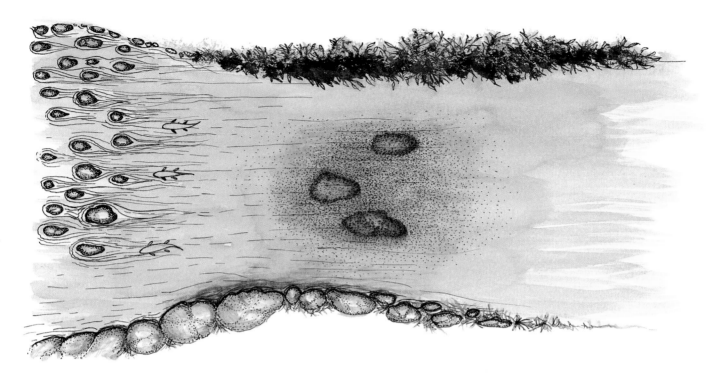

2. Feeding lies.

3. A resting lie.

that are found between the sections of fast water in a stream. There usually are rocks, logs, or other obstructions that create some surface disturbance, but overall, the surface is unbroken. The soft-water sections provide many resting lies, nearly always some feeding lies, and perhaps a few primary lies (Fig. 4).

This is the water fished most often, because it looks like the ideal spot for trout and it's the easiest water in which to wade and fish. You only have to look at the paths along any heavily fished stream to see that it's the *only* water that many anglers fish. The path goes from pool to pool, often swinging wide of any flat fast water, pocket water, or sections of riffles.

Fast Water

Flat Fast Water

Flat fast water is the water in the stream that is moving fast enough for its surface to be broken, although the surface disturbance is not caused by obstructions showing above the surface. This water appears in two types: deep fast water and shallower riffles. The two types differ greatly in their fishability. We'll talk about deep fast water here and discuss riffle water a little later.

Deep Fast Water

Although trout will be found in deep fast water, it's the least productive water type and the most difficult to fish successfully. Any underwater obstructions will provide resting lies for the trout, but it is often difficult to see where those spots are. Likewise, feeding lanes and their adjacent lies are hard to discern. The fast water also makes it hard to make a good presentation of our fly either on or beneath the surface. In short, it's the

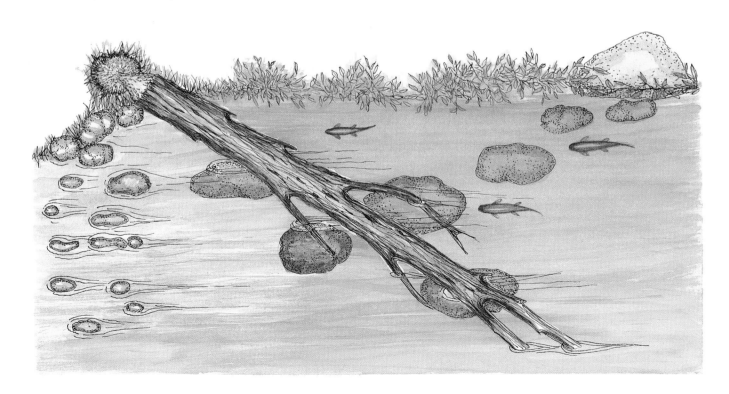

4. Soft water.

5. Deep fast water.

most difficult water to read and fish successfully (Fig. 5).

Pocket Water
Pocket water is fast water whose surface is broken primarily by obstructions (usually rocks) that extend above the surface (Fig.6). Pocket water is passed over by many flyfishers, but, although it is difficult water to fish, it is usually very productive. The rocks and obstructions that break up the stream's flow provide excellent feeding lies, with an abundance of food. It also furnishes a few good resting lies for the trout, but only a few, because there's usually little overhead protection. You may find an occasional primary lie in pocket water, but they're few and far between.

The rapid flow in pocket water makes these sections in the stream challenging for you to fish effectively, but here we can identify the likely lies of the trout, unlike flat fast water.

Riffle Water
Riffle water is moderately fast water whose surface is evenly broken. There may be a few obstructions exposed, but they are basically gravelly runs (Fig.7). This is a highly productive water type that is passed by many anglers because they believe it's too shallow to hold trout. More about this later.

Edges
The most consistent truth in the inconsistent world of flyfishing is that trout feed on *edges*. Some of those edges are readily identifiable. Obviously, where the stream meets the bank is an edge; where the river runs against an obstruction is also an edge.

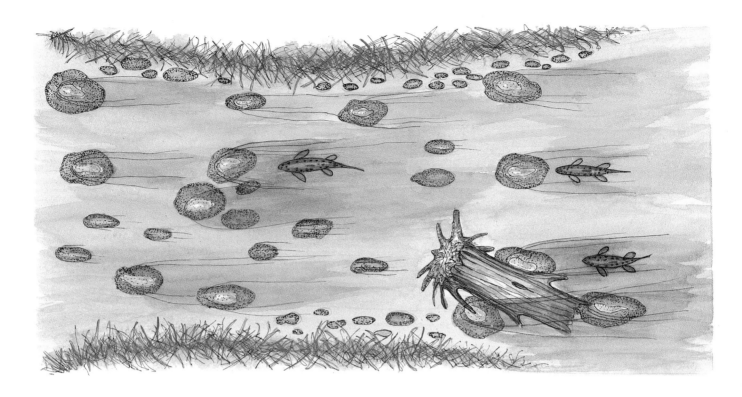

6. Pocket water.

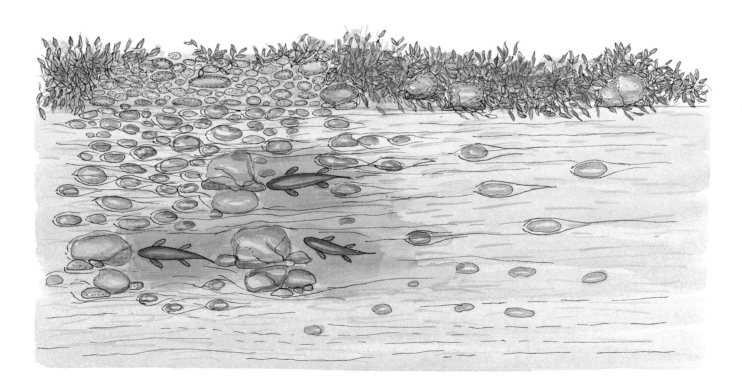

7. Riffle water.

The natural motion of flowing water is not just straight downstream, but also towards the side. Consequently, any food that is present in fast water is pushed towards the edge, where it meets slower water. Edges are productive because they provide an opportunity for the trout to hold in the quieter water, just out of the faster flow, without expending much energy, and to have a lot of food brought within easy reach.

Some edges, however, are a bit more difficult to detect. That narrow run of fast water that causes such a drag problem when we're trying to get a smooth drift represents two edges, one on each side, where its flow is moving past the slower water.

An often overlooked edge is the place where the water meets the stream bottom. Nymph fishers will vouch for the fact that they take the most fish when they are down where they can feel the weight on the leader ticking the bottom. That's partly because the fly is down where the nymphs live, but also because all of those underwater rocks, weeds, logs, or whatever form myriad edges where the trout can hold easily and be presented with a lot of food.

Spring Runoff

Like many western rivers, the Arkansas has a heavy spring runoff-from mid-May into late June and sometimes into July. While the white-water rafters are in their glee, we're left with fishing only along the river-bank. It's just as well, because only a fool wades out into that maelstrom of heavy water, replete with logs and other life-threatening debris, not to mention the flotilla of rafts.

Most of the obstructions in the center of the river are completely covered with water; thus, there aren't a lot of edges out there for the trout to hold along. They move in to the shore edge, where the water flow is a little gentler and the water is shallow enough that rocks are exposed, creating a multitude of edges. Almost the entire fishable river is pocket-water fishing. On the positive side, the fish are more congregated than later in the summer, when they can spread out over the entire river. They also seem to be feeding heavily coming out of their winter of slowed activity, and the combination makes for some exciting fishing.

Meadow streams also experience runoff as the snow melts up in the mountains, with the river often coming out of its banks. Wading can be treacherous, because you can't tell clearly where the bank ends and the normal channel of the stream starts. The river flow undercuts the banks, and every once in a while the solid earth under your feet collapses and you're in the river to your waist. It's all worth it, though, because the fishing can be great.

Fishing the edges takes on new meaning here. Often the trout are holding back under the cut banks, out of the main flow of the river, and your fly has to be presented right on the edge. Not 6 inches from the grass, not 3 inches from the edge, but *right on the edge.*

High water or low; heavy, fast water or soft, *fish the edges and you'll find the trout.*

Reading the Water: Tips and Techniques

Many years ago, when I knew even less about trout fishing than I do now, I was on a famed Pennsylvania stream that was alive with feeding trout. There were a few yellowish mayflies on the water, and I had a perfect match (a pert little Light Cahill, as I recall) on my tippet. I cast to dozens of rising trout for 30 minutes and managed only one tiddler of about 6 inches. I changed flies, I tried longer and finer tippets, I changed flies again, I cast upstream, across stream, and downstream. In short, I tried everything I'd read from the experts, to no avail.

My first clue should have been that there were so many rising fish but only a few mayflies on the water. Although the trout were leaving dimples on the surface, things were awful-ly quiet—none of the usual popping sounds that accompany trout taking adults from the surface. It was several years before I came to recognize the signs of nymphing fish, trout taking nymphs just under the surface, whose backs or tails create those dimples on the water (Fig. 8).

We frequently see frenzied flyfishers whipping the stream to a froth with dry flies without success, because the trout are feeding on nymphs just under the surface and are either not seeing, or are ignoring, their surface offerings.

Some of the nymphs do make it past the trout and hatch into adults, which accounts for the few that are on the surface. As the number of emerging nymphs increases, so does the number that actually hatch, until they're in the majority. At about that point, the trout often switch and start feeding on the adults. Consequently, the dry flies start being successful, and the angler quickly forgets about the 20 or 30 minutes of frustration that preceded their success, and nothing has been learned.

That 20 or 30 minutes of fishing nymphs just under the surface can be

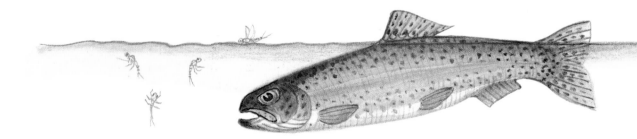

8. Nymphing trout.

more exciting than the hatch itself. Don't let the opportunity get away!

If what you're doing isn't resulting in some action, you need to change what you're doing. That doesn't necessarily mean you should go to a smaller fly, or lengthen your leader, or add finer tippet. The answer may lie in any one of those or a dozen other solutions, but you don't have time to randomly try them all.

We still get fooled occasionally by this "false hatch," because we are always hoping that we'll find ourselves in the midst of a flurry of hatching activity, but we don't stay fooled very long. We've learned that when things aren't happening as they should, it's time to slow down and look around at what's going on. Do you hear rising fish? Are there enough adult insects on the surface to warrant the activity you're seeing? Do you see any birds over the water? Has the sun popped out or gone behind clouds?

Don't ignore riffle water. Most anglers are too quick to walk past riffle water on their way to the next pool. They usually discount it as being too shallow to hold trout of any size. They're dead wrong. We frequently amaze clients by having them take nice trout out of this seemingly too shallow water. In fact, we're sometimes amazed ourselves at how many average and better fish are present in this ankle-deep water.

Wade slowly up through a section of riffle water (fish it first), and you'll find dozens of places where the fast-moving water has washed out hollows among and behind rocks. These hollows are often calf-deep, plenty of depth to hold a nice fish. Even the rocks that are completely underwater create edges, and edges mean a concentration of food. If there's a comfortable place to hold and a heavy food supply, you can bet trout will be there.

Preparing for a hatch. It sure is wonderful when the weather and water conditions are just right and you get into one of those hatches that lasts for several hours. The insects are hatching sporadically, frequently enough that the trout continue looking up, but in small enough numbers that they don't get gorged and quit feeding. Yes, it's nice, but it's not the norm. Most hatches are pretty short-lived, so you have to make the most of the opportunity.

It's a rare flyfisher that isn't anticipating a hatch coming off any time he or she is on the stream. You don't want to miss part of it because you aren't prepared. Check your leader for wind knots, make sure your tippet is right, find which pocket the fly box is in that holds your dry flies, and answer the call of nature if it's necessary.

After the hatch has started isn't the time to decide that you need a longer or finer or heavier tippet. It's not the time to clean your line or patch your waders, and it's not the time to be at the car tying up a few flies or searching for your other fly box—it's the time to catch fish. Be ready for it!

Learn and remember. A good memory is one of the angler's greatest assets (even if the memories "grow" over time). Do you really think your guide just has an uncanny sense of exactly where to cast, what fly to use, and what water *not* to fish? Well, most guides have developed a good sense of such things, but that sense is formed by memory—if not of this exact piece of water, then memory of a piece of water similar to it. Guides pick up information about fly selection, holding lies of the trout, intricacies of the currents, and a whole bagful of information from the last client they fished this stretch with…and the client before that…and the one before that….

It takes a little mental discipline to consciously put the facts into your memory bank, but it's worth the effort. If you're going to fish this section of river again, it has a very direct payback. If you're not likely to revisit, you are likely to fish similar places. The ability to recall what you've learned here will be of real benefit.

Learning from friends. There's a group of four to six of us that get together once a year for a week of intense fishing. We stay in a building (lovingly referred to as "the shack") we built some years ago on Don's property to house our flyfishing schools. It's rustic, to say the least. No electricity, no running water, but with a breathtaking view from the outhouse, and it's only a 5-minute walk to the river.

The camaraderie is great, and some of the stories told by lantern light are…well, let's just say that none of them are made lesser in the telling. Over the years, we've settled into a unique style of fishing that is as educational as it is fun.

We break up into groups of two or three, and each group shares a section of the river. It goes like this: Steve gets in the water and proceeds to fish through a stretch of water while Mace and I watch, kibitz, and needle. Steve fishes until either (1) he takes a fish, or (2) he misses a fish, at which point he comes out and Mace goes in for his turn, and so on.

It's a lot of fun with the right companions (and why fish with any other kind?), but most important, you learn so much. You get to really watch and evaluate another's casting and presentation. The two watchers start comparing notes on reading the water and get to see if their ideas of where the trout are holding are accurate. You quickly find which flies are and aren't working, usually with some thoughtful discussion as to why, and you begin to

9. A reverse eddy.

better grasp all the details of this complex pursuit.

Meanwhile, Don, Lance, and Slaton are on another section of the river, doing the same thing. When we all get back at the shack for lunch, or at the end of the day, there are stories to be told on one another and truths to be stretched, but, more important, a lot of information to be shared about what was seen and learned. We've all become better flyfishers as a result.

I wouldn't want to only fish this way. There are times when I want to be alone with the river and the trout, but by March of each year, we're all sure looking forward to that week at the shack!

The next time you're out with a friend, try this method of fishing for at least a half day instead of each of you going off on your own. You'll be surprised at how much you both learn; maybe it will become a favored way of yours to share the river on occasion.

Fast water into slow water. Look for places in the stream where food is concentrated. The most obvious of these are where fast water enters slow water, as at the head of a pool. The water above the pool is usually moving fast, because it is coming through a narrower section; all of the food in the water is compressed into this reduced cross section. When that fast water enters a slower section, that concentration of available food is dispersed into a relatively small area of quieter water. If the trout are feeding, there will be some in that area, taking advantage of the increased amount of food available.

Reverse eddies. Reverse-flowing eddies along the edges of the stream are formed in sharp bends and where an obstruction extends out into the water (Fig. 9). These, too, are quiet waters where above-average quantities of food collect. They sometimes provide a lot of overhead protection also; then they're often primary lies. Look for trout there.

Cold water and springs. A trout's metabolism slows way down when the water temperature is low. You'll practically have to put the fly in its mouth to have any success. Cold water, at its normal level, usually means that you'll have to get your fly right down on the bottom. In these conditions, you should work through the water pretty quickly. The trout will be inclined to school up in choice spots; large sections of the river may be devoid of

fish. Covering a lot of water gives you a greater chance of finding the places where they are congregated. When you find the fish, though, you need to cover that water in a tighter pattern than you might in warm weather, because they won't move the couple of feet to take your fly as they will in warm water.

Often, feeder streams and springs are several degrees warmer than the main river in the winter, and the trout will gather in the first suitable area below where the feeder comes in— one where there is cover and reduced water flow. One of the sections that we fish on the Arkansas has several warm springs that trickle into the river; the pockets just below them are always choice spots to find trout during the cold months.

Hot days, warm water, and snow melt. Trout activity also slows down when the water temperature gets too high. On bright, sunny days, the structures in the stream accumulate a lot of solar energy in the form of heat and release that heat into the water. It's not unusual for water temperatures to increase 8 or 10 degrees Fahrenheit between sunrise and sunset.

Small flows, particularly if from springs, are generally cooler than the stream in the summer (just as in the winter they're warmer than the stream), and trout will tend to settle into lies just downstream from where the spring water enters the river.

As incredible as it sounds, we've found that on hot summer days, water temperatures will actually *decrease* in many mountainous streams! The hot weather increases the rate of snow melt up in the mountains, and that influx of cold water actually lowers the temperature of the water in the river. Where the snow melt flows into the river is often a real glory hole. Don't pass one up—in fact, they're worth searching out.

Oxygen in water. Warm water carries less oxygen than cool water. When water temperatures get high, the trout frequently move up into riffles and pocket water, where the tumbling water has a higher oxygen concentration.

As you can see, reading water isn't just about observing the structure of the stream. You need to be aware of the trout's physical requirements, the effects of weather on the stream, the influence of water levels on the trout, and a hatful of other things that influence the trout's behavior. Some of these you can learn from books and

more experienced flyfishers, but many of them you'll have to pick up from experience. Don't forget to put them in your memory bank.

Phil Camera

Study the water. A lot of valuable information can be obtained by taking a few minutes before fishing to study the water you are about to approach. Subjects to consider are:

1. Safety
2. Fishy spots
   • Feeding lanes (confined current flow)
   • Pocket water (downstream side of large rocks)
   • Oxygenated water (shallow rapids)
   • Thermal fluctuations (spring or feeder stream entering)
3. Casting position to get proper drift.

Al Diem

Visualize underwater structure. When you don't have rising fish showing you their location, you have to visualize the underwater structure of the river to get the best idea of where the resting, feeding, and prime lies are. You can develop your ability to visualize the underwater structure by taking the time to really study the relationship between the water's surface and the underlying geography when you happen on an area where the light is such that you can clearly see below the surface. By consciously making the connection between structure and water surface variations, you will develop a storehouse of knowledge that will let you more accurately judge the underwater character during the majority of the time, when you can't see beneath the surface.

Wading through a stretch of water after fishing it will also help you establish some correlation between surface disturbances and their underwater sources. It needs to be done as a conscious effort, though, so that the tidbits of information get stored away in your memory bank.

Jerry Gibbs

Places to find fish. Sure, the deep pools and log jams hold the larger trout, but those spots receive concentrated angling pressure, too. You'll catch more, even if smaller, fish by working less obvious undercut banks (even those with low ceilings), deep slots, thick weed beds, rock ledges, rock cave mouths, and boulders. They'll hold browns and brookies. Rainbows are likely to be in the faster shelving water and cuts formed by current junctions.

Early spring flies. In the very early spring, trout in lakes typically key on forage fish in the morning; then, once sated, they move to rocky coves to rest.

Here they'll take the occasional crayfish. In the afternoon, they'll work the rocks, especially where wind-driven waves cause turbulence. Your fly needs to be on the bottom and a dark green color.

Lake ice-out. Lake ice-out is a traditional time to fish near inlets, where trout target spawning forage fish like smelt. Early in the morning, instead of starting right at the mouth, begin working 50 yards (46 m) or more off the tributary. Larger trout are often here, because by first light the forage fish have dropped from the stream and spread out into the inlet.

Predawn feeding. Browns in many northern areas have two special predawn feeding patterns from late spring through early fall. Some large browns will be in the extreme shallows, eating minnows, other·trout, or crayfish. Let your streamer dead drift, since a nervous retrieve will spook the big fish. Second, be aware of the drift effect. That's when caddis, mayflies, and stoneflies let go of the bottom and drift downcurrent before anchoring themselves again. Just before daybreak, trout have a brief window of time to see and nail these easy riders. The free lunch ends at dawn.

Joan Wulff

A water sock. You can gather sound information about the flow of water at various levels and relative to the obstructions for the best lies for trout by using a water sock, much as a pilot uses a wind sock to determine wind velocity and direction.

Make an instant water sock by attaching a 1-foot-long (30 cm) piece of brightly colored yarn to your rod tip. Carry the yarn in your vest, and fish a pool on your favorite river. Take note of any spot in the pool where you see a rise, catch a fish, or see any other sign of a trout's being there. When you have finished fishing, tie on the yarn and go to each of the places you noted. Dip your rod into the water where the trout was, to see the effect of the flow on your water sock. Then look at the surface for signs of how to identify this ideal speed. Now use this knowledge

to explore the rest of the pool to learn the differences between the surface signs of good and bad lies.

The water sock will indicate the velocity and direction of the flow. Move around the pool from one side to the other and down through to the tail, dipping the yarn behind rocks, moving it slowly from top to bottom in the deepest areas, and letting it identify eddies. You will see a change in the yarn's behavior with each new circumstance. When you have gone all the way through the pool, you'll have a database to which you can add by using your water sock in other kinds of water such as pocket water, riffles, runs, and seams. The hands-on experience will be more valuable than all of the descriptions of perfect water flow you'll ever read and, at the very least, it will make what you read more understandable.

Casting and Presentation

The Basics

There are thousands of variations on the basic fly cast, and an experienced caster probably uses hundreds of those variations in a day on the stream. The key point, however, is that all of the casts are *variations* on the basic cast. We'll limit the discussion of the basic casts to only three: the tight loop, the wide loop, and the roll cast. We'll discuss the other variations in the Tips and Techniques section of the chapter.

The major point of understanding is that we cast the fly line, not the fly. The fly arrives at its destination because it's attached to the leader and the fly line.

Since the fly line has considerable weight, the rod will flex anytime it's moved against that weight. The rod, then, tries to return to its original straight configuration. The bend in the rod represents stored energy; it's that energy that you use to throw or cast the fly line. The only force required of the caster is to move the rod against the weight of the line. Flycasting, done

1. The backcast.

correctly, doesn't require a lot of strength or effort. What it does require, though, is that you time the storing and releasing of that energy so that it is imparted to the fly line through the leader and, ultimately, to the fly.

Basic Casting Stroke

Let's walk through a basic casting stroke. You have 15 or 20 feet (4½ to 6 m) of line stretched out in front of you on the water and your rod tip is pointed slightly below horizontal. You begin the cast by smoothly and quickly raising the rod tip to just past vertical. As you move the rod against the

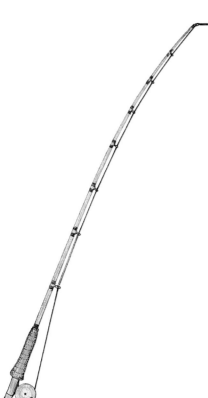

2. The forward cast.

weight of the line, it bends, and energy is stored in it. In raising the rod to vertical, you also began moving the line up and backward.When you stop the rod, it straightens out, throwing the line higher and behind you.

The line will form a candy-cane shape (called the rolling loop) in the air as it goes past the rod tip, which is still stopped just past vertical. The loop will smoothly unroll until the line is straight out behind and slightly above you in the air. You've just made a pickup (lifting the line off the water) and a backcast (Fig. 1).

If, while the line is still straightened out in the air, you begin returning the rod toward its original horizontal position, the weight of the line will again flex the rod, and the line will start moving in the direction you're facing. The line will form another rolling loop as it passes the rod tip and continues to unroll out in front of you.

Notice that the rod is moved towards the original horizontal position. If you move the rod all the way to horizontal, you'll be aiming the line down at the water, which won't allow time for the loop to unroll completely, and you'll make a big splash on the water. The rod tip is stopped about 60 degrees above horizontal or, visualizing the hands on a clock, at about the 1 o'clock position. This keeps the *line* moving forward, parallel to the surface of the water, and allows time for the loop to completely unroll before gravity pulls it to the water's surface. You've just made a forward cast (Fig. 2).

We've taught hundreds of people to flycast. Every single one of them has made the same two mistakes over and over, until we've almost come to believe those are the only two things you can do wrong! So here is Reminder Number One: The rod has to stop just past vertical (at the 11 o'clock position) on the backcast. People stop their arms at the right position and then bend their wrists so that the rod tip is horizontal or below horizontal behind them. This aims the unrolling loop right at the water behind them and doesn't allow time for the loop to unroll before gravity pulls it into the water. Remember, the *rod* stops at 11 o'clock on the backcast.

Reminder Number Two: It takes time for the line to unroll behind you once you've stopped the rod at 11 o'clock. That means you have to wait before you start moving the rod forward into the forward cast. That's wait…as in STOP, don't move. Of course, if you wait too long, gravity will win out and your line will be on the water before you start forward. You want to start the forward motion just as the tip of the line enters the unrolling loop.

Both of these persistent problems can be solved by the simple act of looking back over your shoulder as you complete the backcast. If the rod's not in your field of vision, it's because you've bent your wrist and the rod is straight out behind you. You can watch the line unroll and start your forward cast just as the tip of the line enters the

rolling loop. That's all it takes to handle both problems but, for some reason, it's hard to get beginners to take that look over their shoulders. The look over the shoulder isn't just for beginners, either. Those of us who've been at it for a while sometimes check our backcasts in this way to see the effect of the wind and to make sure the area behind is clear for the backcast before we hang our fly up in a tree.

Loop Control

Tight Loop

We can make the two basic casts from the basic casting stroke: the tight loop and the wide loop.

The tight loop is the most basic of the two and is the stroke you use nearly all of the time. The tight loop has a rolling loop that is very narrow when measured from top to bottom (Fig. 3). Because the tight loop decreases the radius of the unrolling loop, the line must move faster around the tighter curve and thus unrolls faster—what we call increased line speed. The faster the line unrolls, the less time gravity has to pull the line toward the water. This becomes critical on long casts, where there is more line to unroll before gravity takes its toll. The tight loop, with its narrower leading edge, also presents less surface area into a headwind and punches through the wind. With less distance between the top and bottom of the loop, it also isn't affected as much by a wind from the side as a wider loop is.

A tight loop is accomplished by keeping the rod tip as high as possible throughout the forward cast. You should move the butt of the rod forward *parallel to the water* as long as possible. This means that you make the forward cast by pushing your hand straight out, as if throwing a punch. When you've pushed the rod out as far as you can reach, your wrist will automatically snap forward and lower the rod tip slightly so it is clear of the unrolling line.

The technique of keeping the line in the air through a series of forward and back casts is called false-casting; it serves several purposes. You can adjust the length of your line by feeding out or working in some line with your left hand (for a right-handed caster). You can judge where your fly is going to land by watching the line unroll on the forward cast. You can see the effect of the wind on your forward cast and adjust your aim to compensate, and, if you're fishing a dry

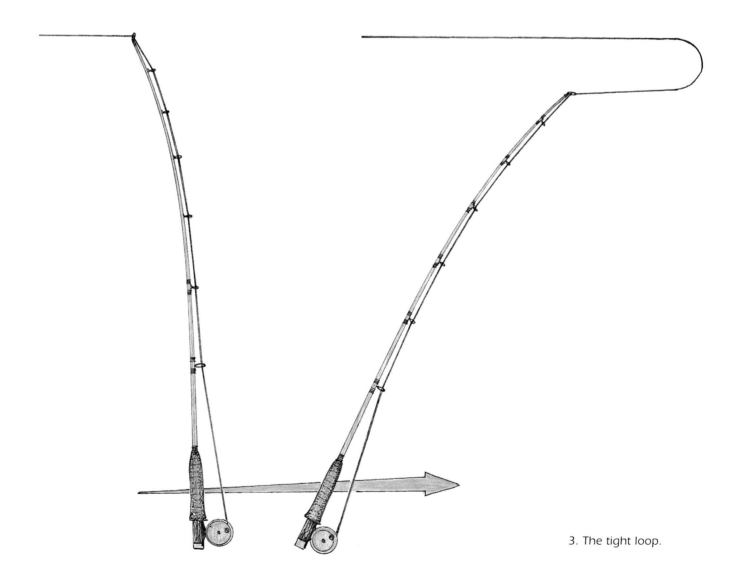

3. The tight loop.

fly, false-casting will dry the fly. The tight loop is the cast used for false-casting and consequently is your most used cast.

Wide Loop

Because the tight loop unrolls the line so quickly, it is difficult to make a delicate presentation of the fly on the water. The rapid turnover of the leader will usually cause the fly to slap down on the water and create a lot of distur-

bance. To avoid this problem, we generally use a wide loop on the last forward cast to soften the landing of the line, leader, and fly.

The wide loop is created by simply moving the tip of the rod down towards the water on the forward cast (Fig. 4). This pulls the bottom section of the rolling loop away from the top section, slows the line speed and, done correctly, will leave just enough line speed to barely straighten out the

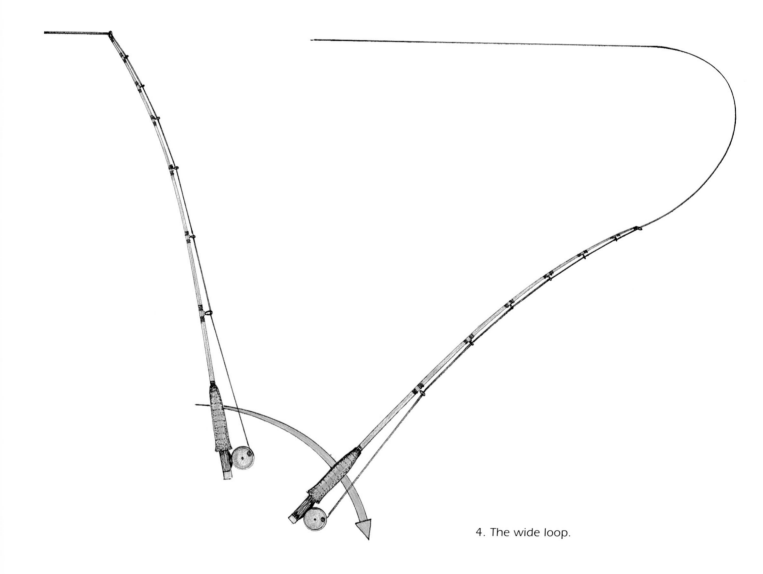

4. The wide loop.

leader before it and the fly drop to the water. Even though the wide loop is used to *complete* most presentations of a dry fly, the vast majority of your casts should be made using the tight loop.

Roll Cast

There are times when you can't move into a position that allows room for a backcast. The answer is the roll cast. To make the roll cast, you must have some line already on the water. Often, there is room for a short backcast, so you can get some line on the water to start. Barring that, you may have to work out some line by switching the rod from side to side and feeding some line out with each forward motion.

You begin the roll cast with the rod pointing slightly down at the water. Very slowly, start lifting the rod tip. *Slowly;* you don't want to pick the line up from the water, you want it sliding towards you on the surface. Continue slowly raising the rod tip until it's at the 11 o'clock position, and then very quickly move the rod tip forward and down with gusto. You will form a rolling loop, moving away from you right at the tip of the rod (Fig. 5). As that rolling loop continues away from you, it will pick up the line from the water and unroll it out in front of you. A good caster can make some pretty long roll casts, but you don't have the advantage of false-casting to judge your distance and dry your fly. A roll

5. The roll cast.

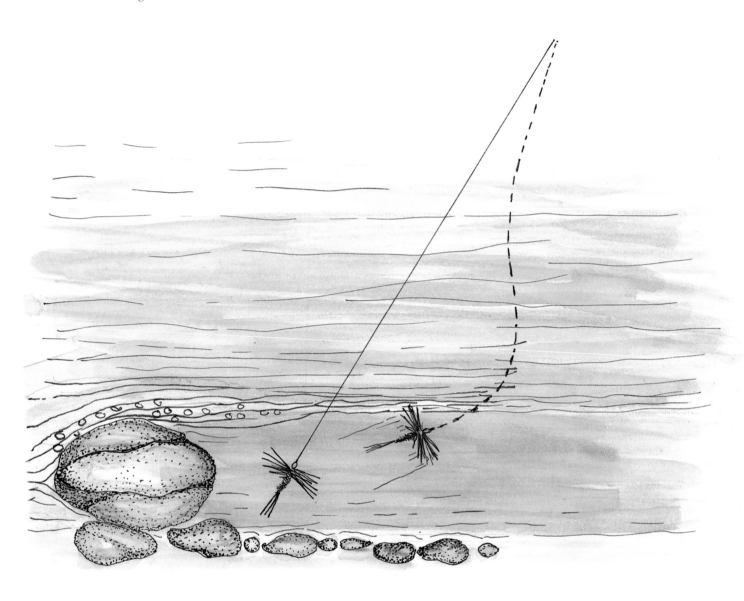

6. Drag.

cast also creates a quite a bit of surface disturbance; consequently, its use is pretty well limited to those cases where your casting room is restricted.

Casting and Presentation: Tips and Techniques

Drag

Let's take a look at a common problem we all experience on the stream when fishing dry flies. There's a hatch coming off and the trout are feeding pretty freely, but most of the rises are across the stream from you. If you make your normal cast up and across the stream, there's a run of fast water between you and the rising fish, which sweeps your line downstream faster than the fly is moving and, of course, the moving line pulls the fly across the stream towards you. Normally, even a heavily feeding trout won't give a second look at a fly demonstrating such an unnatural movement. This unnatural movement is called drag, and it's one of the frustrations of fishing the dry fly.

You need to make a cast that will allow the fly to drift to the fish before the downstream belly in the line can affect it. Essentially, what you need to do is to either put enough slack on the water for the faster current to only move the slack line while your fly drifts naturally into position, or make a cast that lands the fly downstream from the fly line so that the fly gets to the feeding fish before the current pulls it across the stream (Fig. 6). There are several techniques that will solve the problem for you.

S-Cast

You can create some slack on the water by making an S-cast. Just when you've stopped the rod at the completion of your presentation, shake the rod tip sideways as the line is falling to the water. This will create a series of S's in the line on the water (Fig. 7). Now the current will have to straighten out all of that slack before it can start pulling your fly off of its natural drift line. A couple of tips follow to make it work effectively. First, make your presentation cast with a tight loop so that the line will unroll quickly high above the water to give yourself time to make the S's while the line is falling to the surface. Second, cast a longer line to get the fly to land in the right spot to start the drift, because you'll be using some line length to form the S's on the water.

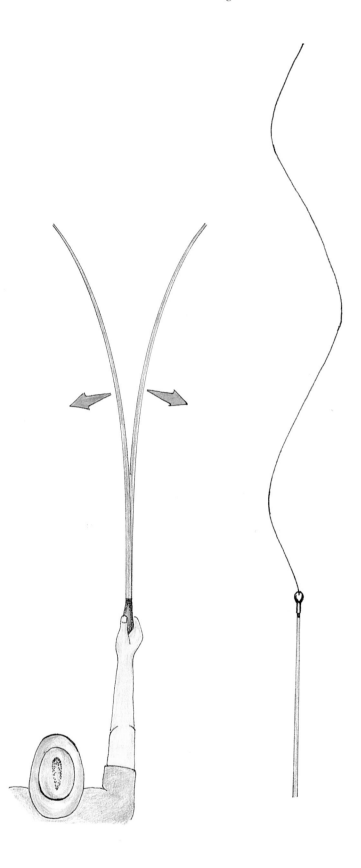

7. The S-cast.

Stop Cast

Another way to create the needed slack is to use a stop cast. Make your presentation cast with a tight loop, and make the cast with a lot of extra force. The line will unroll very quickly high above the water. Because of the extra force you imparted to the cast, the line will straighten out and bounce back towards you as it's falling, creating a quite a bit of slack on the water. Just as with the S-cast, you'll need to cast a long enough line to compensate for the slack you've created on the water (Fig. 8). The stop cast is easier to make than the S-cast, but it's more difficult to judge the line length you need to land the fly in the right position.

You'll also find the S-cast and stop cast invaluable in those cases where you need to make a downstream presentation of your dry fly. If the trout you're after is nearly straight downstream from you, you need to make a cast that will get the fly to the fish before the line gets there. You can use the S-cast or stop cast to put enough slack on the water to drift the fly to the fish.

Line length is critical in this scenario. You have to have enough line on the water for the fly to get all the way to the fish, but not so much that you can't get the slack out to set the hook when the fish takes the fly. The only way to accurately judge the distance is to false-cast, but since the trout is downstream from you, it's looking in your direction, and the motion of your fly line over its head while you're false-casting will spook it. One trick is to cast sidearm so that the line is closer to the water and thus more likely out of the trout's cone of vision. The other thing to do is to cast diagonally across the stream while you're judging distance and then make your presentation cast on line with the feeding fish.

There are times and places where a downstream drift is the only way to get the fly to the trout or, in some cases, the only presentation where the

8. The stop cast.

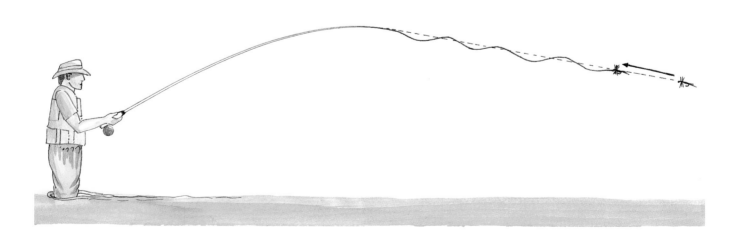

trout will "buy" your offering as a natural insect. Getting the fly to the trout isn't too difficult with an S-cast or stop cast, but hooking up solidly after the take is a little tougher.

When you make a normal up-and-across presentation and the trout takes the fly, the action of tightening the line and raising the rod tip pulls the fly into the trout's lip or jaw, because it's facing away from you. When you make a downstream drift to the fish, the act of setting the hook tends to pull the fly right back out of its mouth, because it's facing towards you. The trick here is patience. Hesitate for just a moment before tightening up on the trout. Immediately after taking your fly, the trout will tip its nose down and usually turn slightly in the current. If that's the moment you set the hook, you'll either hook it in the top jaw or in the corner of the mouth.

Puddle Cast

There are several spots in the areas that we fish where the river comes around a sharp rock point and creates a backward-flowing eddy behind the point. The dilemma here is that, although you're facing upstream, this little piece of water is running away from you. These eddies are often prime lies for the trout, because they're well protected and a lot of food is moved past them by the swirling current. The slack line technique called for here is the puddle cast, which puts the majority of the line on the water in a pile. The fly, leader, and end of the line drift down

the back-flowing eddy and simply pull the needed line from the pile as it drifts freely.

The puddle cast is an exaggerated wide-loop cast. You adjust the line length while false-casting so that the fly is turning over 6 or 8 feet (1.8 to 2.5 m) past the end of the run (or the feeding fish, if present), using your normal tight loop. On the presentation cast, you lower the rod tip so that it's pointed at the water only 3 or 4 feet (1 or 1.2 m) away. Lowering the rod tip so drastically really opens up the loop. The line will fall in a pile with the fly, leader, and first few feet of line started downstream.

Chicken Wing

Bob Damico has an additional technique that really works well. We've dubbed it the chicken wing. Instead of just lowering the rod tip on the presentation cast, raise your casting elbow as high as you can, kinda like flapping one wing (Fig. 9). This rolls the rod over, pulls it back towards you slightly as the butt raises, and points the tip at the water just in front of you. The end result is that the casting loop is as wide as we can make it. The loop forms a nearly vertical shape and will fall quietly and neatly, practically at your feet.

We also use the chicken wing occasionally when there's a need to make a very quiet presentation to a rising fish. It's not quite as exaggerated in this case, but if you raise your elbow when making the presentation cast, the loop

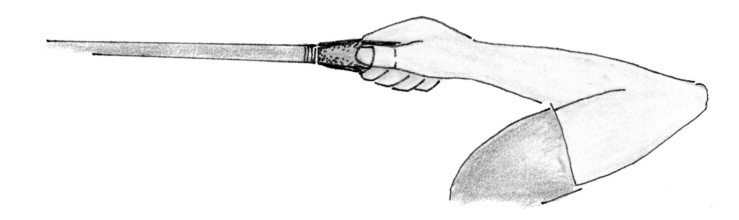

9. *The chicken wing.*

becomes very wide, the line speed is slowed, and the fly lands as delicately as a dandelion puff.

Another way to overcome the problem of an intervening faster current creating drag is to make a cast that places the line upstream from the fly. That way, your fly can drift naturally until the faster current between you and it moves the line downstream past the fly. There are a couple of ways of doing it: the curve cast and the reach cast.

Curve Cast

To make a left-hand curve cast (the fly lands left of the line), you make a tight-loop presentation cast; when your arm reaches full extension, you snap your wrist quickly in a clockwise motion (Fig. 10a). The rotation should take place as part of the normal wrist snap at the end of the casting stroke.

Rotating the loaded rod 90 degrees with your wrist repositions the unrolling loop from the vertical plane to the horizontal plane. If, as the loop unrolls, there is enough power in the cast, the leader and fly will unroll past straight and curl in the opposite direction, creating a curve in the line (Fig. 10b).

The tricks, then, are to make a strong tight-loop cast to generate a lot of line speed and to aim the cast well above the water so that the curve has time to form before falling to the surface. A left curve (as described) is relatively easy for a right-handed caster, and a right curve is easy for a left-handed caster because of the direction of their natural wrist rotation. Although the same technique will throw a curve in the other direction, the needed wrist rotation is in the opposite direction and our wrists just don't move that way as easily.

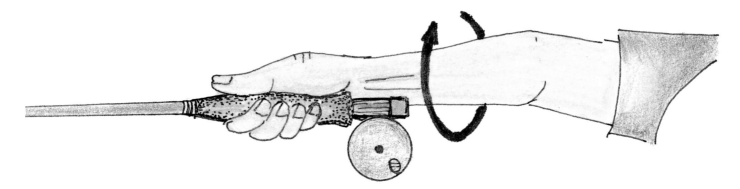

10a. Wrist snap for the curve cast.

10b. The curve cast.

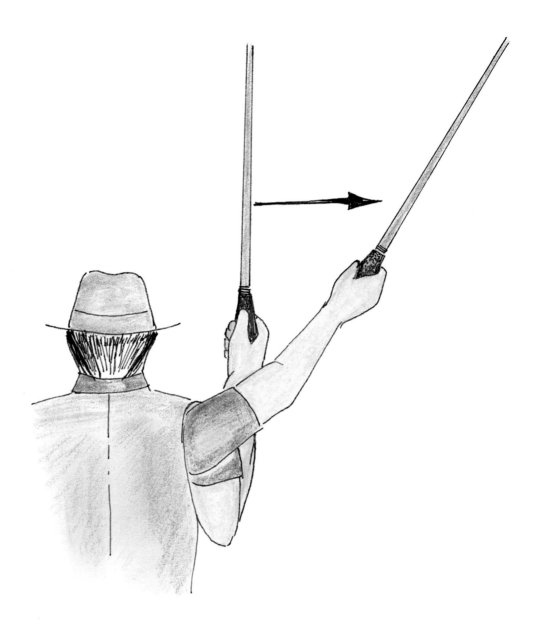

11. The reach cast.

Reach Cast

The reach cast has the advantage over curve casts in that it is easier to master and is equally easy in either direction. You make the reach cast by moving the rod as far left or right (upstream) as you can reach, just as the line straightens out (Fig. 11). When you move the rod, you pull the rod end of the line upstream, and the fly neces- sarily lands downstream from the line. The disadvantage to the reach cast is that you can't get the line as far above the fly as you can with a strong curve cast.

Just as with the curve cast, you need some time to make the rod movement while the line is still in the air, so you should cast a tight loop, aimed well above the water.

Double-Haul Cast

You've probably been there. There's a fish rising steadily 10 feet (3 m) further out than you can reach with your normal cast, and you can't wade any closer. You need a cast that will get you another 10 or 20 feet of distance.

The double-haul is the long-distance cast you're looking for. It generates considerably more power than a normal forward cast by increasing the bend in the rod and storing more energy in it. When that extra energy is released into the forward cast, it really increases the line speed and lets you make a longer cast.

The double-haul is relatively simple in principle, but the timing is critical. It will take a quite a bit of practice for you to be comfortable with it, but it's worth the time spent.

Step 1. Pull some extra line from the reel and allow it to just hang between your line hand (the left hand for right-handed casters) and the reel (Fig. 12). Now, make your normal backcast. You've stopped the rod at the 11 o'clock position while you're waiting for the line to unroll. Up to this point nothing is changed from your normal backcast.

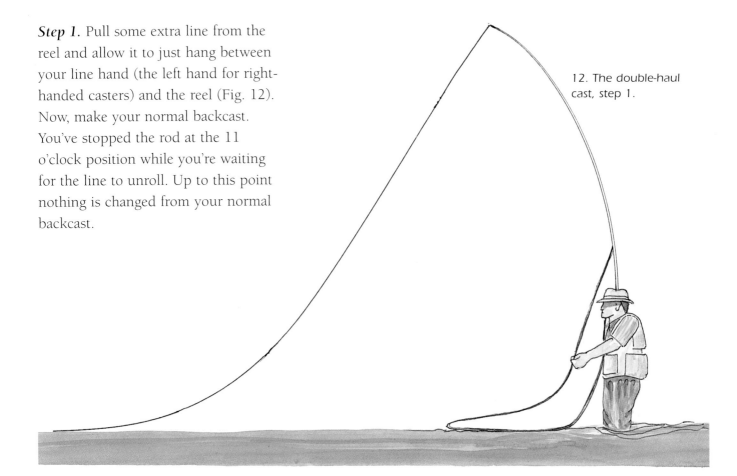

12. The double-haul cast, step 1.

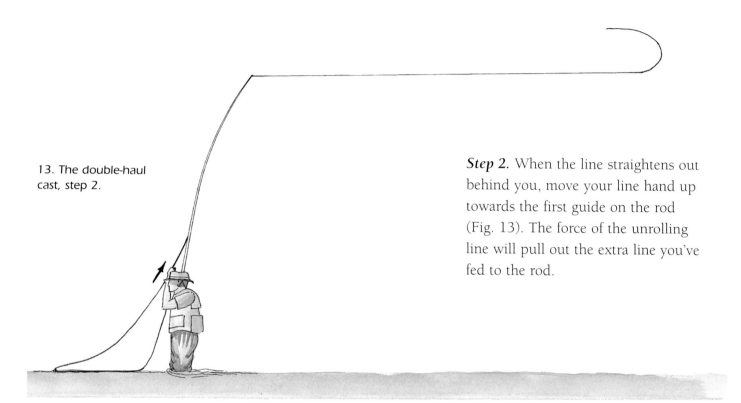

13. The double-haul cast, step 2.

Step 2. When the line straightens out behind you, move your line hand up towards the first guide on the rod (Fig. 13). The force of the unrolling line will pull out the extra line you've fed to the rod.

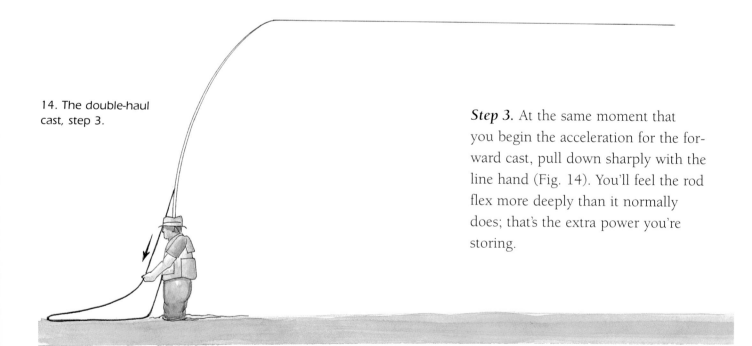

14. The double-haul cast, step 3.

Step 3. At the same moment that you begin the acceleration for the forward cast, pull down sharply with the line hand (Fig. 14). You'll feel the rod flex more deeply than it normally does; that's the extra power you're storing.

Step 4. As the line unrolls in front of you, throw the loop of line you're holding towards the first guide on the rod (Fig. 15). The rapidly unrolling line will pull that extra line into the air, and you will have extended your cast by that distance. Aim your cast a little higher than normal to buy the time you need for the extra line to unroll.

15. The double-haul cast, step 4.

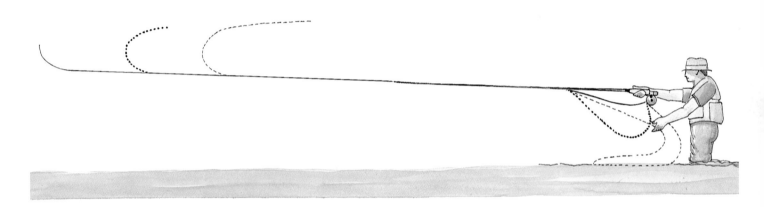

Combating the Wind

I shall stay him no longer than to wish him a rainy evening to read this following discourse: and if he be an honest angler, the east wind may never blow when he goes a fishing.
—*Izaak Walton*

Oh the wind, the bane of the flyfisher! We have all of the line we're using up in the air a great deal of the time and, plain and simple, the wind moves it around—rarely to our liking. If there's a wind parallel to the direction you're casting, it opposes the unrolling of the loop in one direction and assists it in the other. The loop thus takes longer to unroll in one direction than the other, which requires you to adjust your timing differently on each end of the cast. A crosswind plays havoc with your casting accuracy. I can false-cast three or four times to get an aiming point that will offset the effect of the wind, and just as I make my presentation, either the wind stops momentarily or it gusts. We don't count the wind among our friends when we're casting the fly.

There are some ways to partially overcome old Mariah, though. The best defense is the tight loop. It presents a small frontal area to the wind and penetrates well. It increases line speed, and the less time it takes the line to unroll, the less time the wind has to affect it.

work to overcome the problem: the shorter leader is stiffer and will transmit more power to the fly, and the shorter leader needs less time to unroll, giving the wind less time to interfere.

Horizontal cast. Another technique is to change the angle of your cast to a horizontal or nearly horizontal plane. Generally, the wind is weaker close to the surface of the water; the horizontal cast will keep the line down in the quieter air (Fig. 16).

Optimum line length. Although any well-balanced rod-and-line combination will make the whole range of casting distances from short to long, there's an optimum line length at which the weight of the line in the air brings out the best action in the rod. There's a definite advantage to using that line length in windy conditions. This means you may have to spend a little more time moving around to set your casting distance to match that optimum line length, but the effort will be repaid in more accurate and less tiring casting.

Double-haul cast. Although the double-haul cast is primarily used to get increased distance by increasing the line speed and the power of the cast, those same attributes will help you fight a headwind.

Cross-body cast. What do you do when you're on the right side of the river (facing upstream), can't get very far from the shore to clear your back-cast, and the wind's coming from your left? If you make your normal cast, the wind will blow your leader and fly into the brush on the bank. One of my sons is ambidextrous. He simply starts casting left-handed; that's the

Shorter leader. Many times you are able to generate enough power in your cast to get the line to straighten out, but you find that the wind is too strong for the leader to unroll all the way to the fly. Here, you need to cut back your leader. There are two factors that will

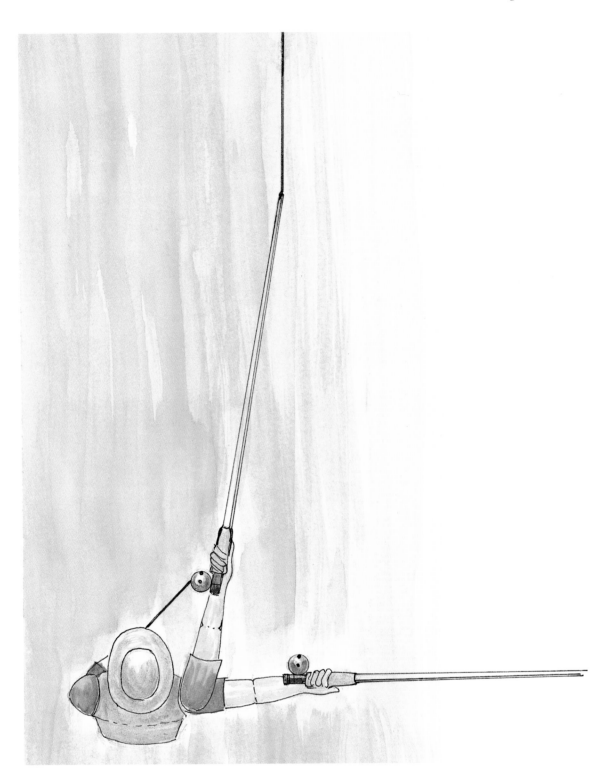

16. The horizontal cast.

best solution. Most of us aren't that lucky; the best we can do is to make a cross-body cast. For a right-handed caster, that means moving your arm across your chest so that the rod is pointing out to the left at about a 45-degree angle; then make a "normal" casting stroke on the left side of your body (Fig. 17). It's not too difficult, but it is tiring.

Wind from your casting-arm side. Another difficult situation occurs when the wind is quartering into you from your casting-arm side. The wind will blow the fly into you on both the forward cast and the backcast. That can be dangerous! The solution: make cross-body casts. With the rod on your left, the wind from the rod-hand side will be blowing the fly away from you as you cast.

Roll-cast pickup. When you're casting nearly straight upstream, into the wind, picking the fly up to start the backcast becomes problematic. As the line comes off the water at the start of

17. The cross-body cast.

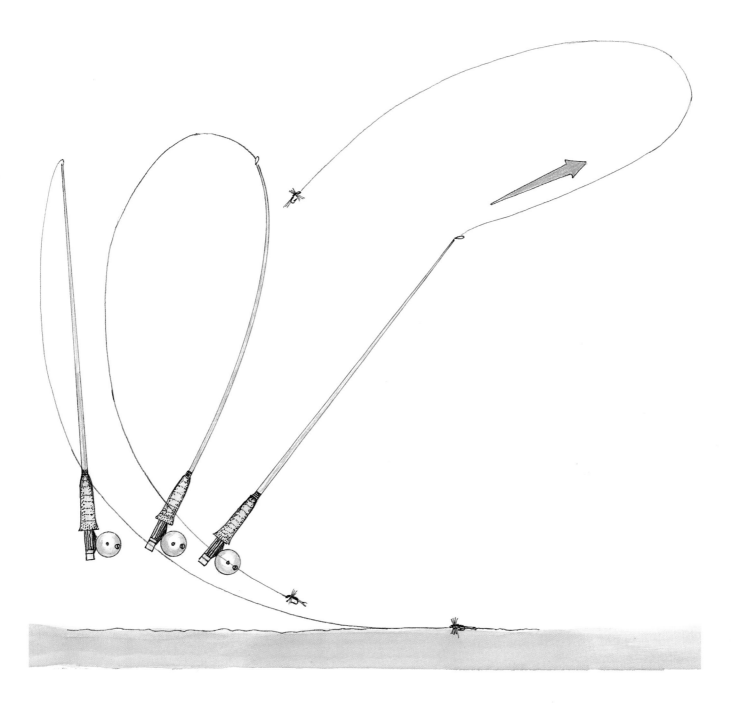

the pickup, the wind blows the leader and fly right back into you. Don put a number #14 Elk-Hair Caddis in his cheek that way a few years back! A roll-cast pickup is the answer.

Raise the rod tip straight up, just as for a regular roll cast, but as you power the rod forward, keep the tip higher than normal, and aim the cast 5 or 6 feet (1.5 to 1.8 m) above the water. The line will come off the water in a rolling loop; you then start your back-cast just as it unrolls (Fig. 18). It all happens pretty quickly, because you only have a short line on the water.

18. The roll-cast pickup.

The roll-cast unhook. Although not a wind-fighting technique, you can use the same type of roll-cast technique to (sometimes) get your fly unhooked from an upstream snag. Let's say you've cast up into a run between some rocks, and as your fly comes around one of the rocks, it catches on a small branch that's lodged there. Your options seem to be to wade up through the pool, spoiling any possibility of taking a trout from there, or to aim your rod at the rock and pull until something gives—your leader breaks, the hook is straightened (ruining a fly), or the branch comes free and skids across the pool, with the same effect as if you waded up there.

Before accepting any of these undesirable alternatives, try this: strip 10 or 15 feet (3 or 4.5 m) of line from the reel and gently shake it out on the water in front of you. Now make a really strong roll cast, aimed high above the water. The roll cast will shoot out away from you, go past the hung-up fly in the air, and then give a smart tug on the fly from the upstream side (Fig. 19). If you hold your mouth just right, and the river gods are smiling on you, the fly will pop free. It doesn't always work, but the success rate is pretty high.

Unsticking a stuck fly. Not that any of us ever casts a fly into trees or brush, but I understand it does happen to some people. Heck, in the wind it could even happen to you or me. The natural tendency when you see your fly headed for that branch is to pull it back as quickly as you can. Wrong move! The fly is going to wrap around

19. The roll-cast unhook.

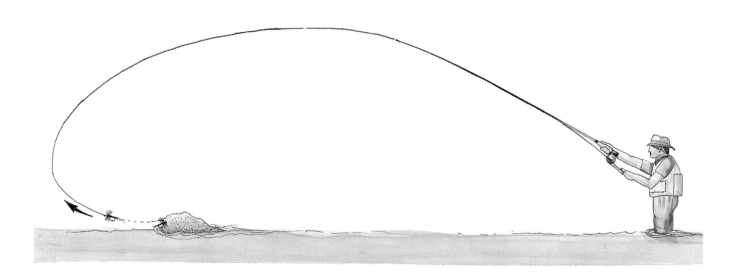

the branch a turn or two and all you're doing is tightening the wrap and making sure the point of the hook finds solid wood. The thing to do is just let it go. Things can't get much worse, so they just might get better.

Many times, the leader will wrap the branch a time or two and then unwind right back off again. Barring that, if you let things settle *softly*, you can then gently pull on the line and the whole thing will sometimes unwind itself. If you've already jerked on it, though, you've tightened up the works and you'll never get it free from where you're standing.

Forward cast in wind. Let's say you're a left-handed caster this time. You're casting a dry fly into a drift line on your right, and there's a strong breeze quartering from the right. The fly drifts down nearly to you and it's time to pick it up for your backcast, but the wind is going to blow the fly right into you. Just let the fly drift on *past* you; then raise your rod and move it over your left shoulder and make a *forward cast* pickup. The wind will blow the line out around you to the left, and you can just continue with your false-casting.

Hat and glasses. That fly on the end of the 20 or 30 feet of line you're casting is sharp, and it hurts when it meets skin. Always wear a hat and glasses when you're flyfishing. Every fly you put into your hat (and we all do occasionally) is one that would be in your person somewhere if the hat weren't in the way. The specter of a fly in your eye is too gruesome to even think about. Wear glasses.

Phil Camera

Grass on the water. A good way to check how your fly is going to ride downstream is to throw a few blades of grass on the water. The grass will ride the same lane as the floating insects, thus identifying the natural feeding lane.

Al Diem

Concentration. The one thing that I see so often as the cause of poor casting performance and, subsequently, less than maximum success is inattention to the cast. Flycasting does settle into a rhythm after a few minutes on the water, and that is the root of the problem. We get so used to the act of casting that we start paying less and less attention to what we're doing with the rod and more and more attention to the drift, and we start missing our target. The solution is to concentrate on each cast with the same degree of intensity that you apply when casting to a rising fish. You'll find that you will spend a lot less time untangling leader messes and getting your fly out of the bushes. You'll also catch more fish in a day of fishing.

Hire a guide. As in skiing, golf, and many other pursuits, your learning curve will be much steeper if you'll spend a few dollars to get some professional help in the beginning. Hire a guide for a half-day and heed well what he or she has to say. Guides make their living flyfishing; they not only know the rivers that they guide on very well, but also know plenty about casting, fly selection, reading the water, and all the other things that go into success. A half-day guide fee is less than the cost of a good-quality fly reel in most areas of the country, and the value of the lessons learned will last even longer.

Practice casting. There should be something akin to golf driving ranges for flycasters. I'll bet that 99 percent of us never cast a fly line except when we're on the water in pursuit of fish. The time on the river will be ever so much more productive if you'll get out and practice before going to the river.

Although this is especially true for the beginner, practicing where we're not distracted with the pursuit of a trout will serve us all well.

Any grassy area will serve as a practice arena. Put out some targets at varying distances and see how quickly you can judge the distance, work out the correct amount of line, and hit the targets. Change your casting position so that the wind is into your face and then coming from behind you; move so that it's quartering into and from behind you. This is the place to learn the double-haul and the curve cast.

No serious golfer (including, *especially,* the pros) ever steps up to the first tee without hitting a few practice balls and spending a few minutes on the putting green; it's a good behavior to emulate.

Teach the other hand. Once you've learned to cast well, it's time to teach the other hand. Cross-body casting is tiring, and accuracy is much harder to achieve when you're on the "wrong" side of the river (the right bank, facing upstream, for a right-hander). It's not difficult to learn to cast with either hand; it will really improve your performance on the stream.

Roll-cast pickup. I know Paul and Don have mentioned the roll-cast pickup before, but this is one technique that I think every flyfisher needs to learn. When the fly is drifting straight down towards you and you try a normal backcast pickup, it will swing right into you when it comes off or out of the water. Just remember to shoot the line out at a high angle so it can unroll well above the water, and then start your backcast quickly. The roll-cast pickup will prevent most of those wind knots that you find in your leader, not to mention a lot of anguish caused by the fly coming towards your face.

Shooting line. When you're fishing upstream and the fly is coming back down towards your position, you are constantly retrieving the slack line. Most flyfishers will then make their pickup and false-cast several times to extend the line back out to its full length. Learn to shoot the line out on one, or at most two, forward casts. This will quickly put the fly back on the water, where there's a chance it will meet up with a willing fish. Shoot more, cast less, and you'll catch more fish. A fly in the air is pretty ineffective!

Feeding rhythm. Ever cast over a rising trout several times without getting a take, even though your fly has been working on other trout quite effectively? Maybe you're just out of sync with its feeding rhythm. Try casting to, and drifting, another area of the stream a time or two; then make your presentation to the riser. By changing the timing between your presentations to the trout, you may catch it when it's back in feeding position and ready to take the next insect that comes by. Keep trying this until you either get it to take your fly or it quits feeding.

Hanging trout. Occasionally, you'll spot a hanging trout, one that is suspended just beneath the surface but doesn't seem to be feeding. Try this technique: make two or three casts so that the fly lands just behind the fish. Don't make a lot of disturbance, but do let the fly land with some commotion. Then make your normal presentation cast 3 or 4 feet (1 or 1.2 m) above the fish—it'll take every time (well, sometimes, anyway).

Jerry Gibbs

Direction of stonefly nymph. When wading and fishing a stonefly nymph, don't work the fly from the bank outward; the real bugs are headed the other way. Instead, cast a weighted nymph short of the shoreline and then mend the line loop beyond the nymph and towards the shore. The current will take the line and angle the fly toward the shore like the real thing.

Slurping trout. Many anglers assume a splashy rise means trout are taking winged adult insects, but fish taking emerging caddis pupae splash just as hard. How do you know which to imitate? Trout plucking adults from the surface take with an audible "slurp" and leave a bubble behind. Trout feeding on emergers or nymphs caught in the surface film may make a splash, but not a bubble. Look for their backs breaking the surface—a sure sign of nymphing trout—if you need further confirmation.

Casting from a drift boat. The biggest mistake you can make when fishing from a drift boat (other than hooking your guide in the nose) is to cast 90 degrees from the boat, straight into the bank. Current, plus the movement of the boat downstream, will instantly rip your fly off target. Also, if your buddy is fishing in the stern, a right-angle cast will block all of his shots. Cast your fly well ahead of the boat.

Movements of rising trout. Predicting the movements of trout rising in lakes as they take insects is an interesting game. When they move in a straight line, it's easy. Most often, though, trout surface in a small area, seemingly without a pattern. However, they typically rise to an insect, take it, and then immediately swirl back. That's why dropping a fly in the ring left on the water from the take is often successful. If there's a breeze, cast upwind of the rise, because the fish will be looking for windswept insects.

Fishing downstream. While wet-fly anglers know how productive fishing downstream can be, too many anglers still stick with the traditional up-current approach when casting dry flies. You'll discover a whole new river when you turn around and work flies back down. Of course, drag can be a greater problem that way, but you'll learn to compensate. You'll be able to reach holding water that was a difficult or impossible off angle for an upstream approach.

Joan Wulff

A bad cast. Even the best anglers make a bad cast now and then. If you are casting to a rising trout and you goof up the cast, don't snatch it off the water in instant response. Your chances of catching that fish will go out the window. Instead, muzzle your emotions and let the line and fly drift right on through the area, and make the next presentation a better one.

Casting with two flies. When you're fishing with two flies on your leader, your casting must be done carefully. To avoid tangling the dropper, don't false-cast to extend length; just pick up the line and put it back down, shooting a little line on each cast, until you've reached the desired distance.

Casting with weight on the leader. Casting with weight on the leader or fly changes everything. You must cast with less force and more slowly and,

on the backcast, wait for the line, leader, and fly to be fully extended before coming forward. Leading the line through a circular or an oval pattern or changing planes between the backcast and forward cast are other good techniques. Another casting alternative is a one-stroke cast. At the end of the fly's drift, lift the weight to the surface; then, turning upstream, reverse your forearm and hand so you can make a forward cast, accelerating very slowly.

Playing and landing a fish. Nine times out of ten, a fish will be hooked on the side of the mouth that was nearest you when it took the fly. Picture the fish facing upstream. As it takes the fly, its connection to you, plus the strike, will move it towards you so it hooks in that side of his jaw. Whenever you land a fish, check to see if this is true. This knowledge can be important in the playing and landing of a big fish: you cannot put maximum pressure on it from any side but the one on which it is hooked without the danger of pulling or working the hook out of its mouth.

chapter five

Wading

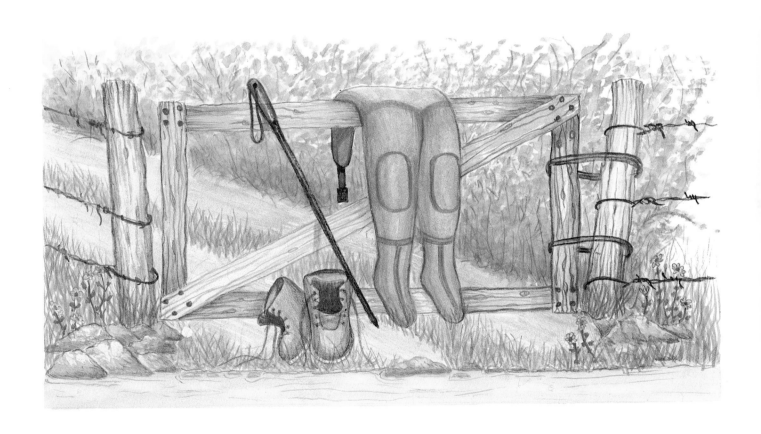

The Basics

Wading in moving water has some inherent dangers. Every year a few anglers drown while fishing, but the level of risk is small if you bring just a modicum of knowledge and your good sense to the stream.

Waders

One of the real frustrations of teaching new flyfishers is that they so often show up without waders of any sort. The most classic case we have experienced in our flyfishing schools were the three people who studied our school brochure thoroughly, saw that they needed boots, and went out and purchased some. They arrived at the school equipped with brand new snow boots! Waders are relatively expensive. They seem to be the one thing that newcomers to the sport think they can get by without. It's just not so, unless you're willing to wade wet—"blue-leggin' it," it's called in our part of the country. Whoever is teaching you can probably come up with a rod, reel, and line that you can use; in a pinch, the two of you can share one outfit; but it's awfully hard to share a pair of waders.

Let's dispel a myth. If you fall and your waders fill up with water, they will *not* pull you down to the bottom of the stream. The density of the water inside and outside of the waders is the same—water doesn't have weight in water. When you try to exit from the water, however, the water inside the

waders weighs a lot, which can make getting out difficult. That's why you should wear a wading belt. The wading belt isn't going to keep you from getting quite wet, but it will decrease the amount of water that gets into your waders and might make getting out of the river much easier.

Falling In

Wading isn't a walk in the park. There are holes to step into, rocks to trip over, mud to sink in, and weeds to trip you up. There are going to be times when you stumble and probably a time or two when you fall, so be ready for it to happen. The opportunity for injury to both body and equipment is increased greatly by the struggle to avoid falling. I've seen many anglers perform a passable rendition of the *Danse Macabre* (as our friend Bob Damico always calls it) as they twist and turn, leaping from one precarious rock perch to the next, with equipment bouncing in all directions, only to increase their forward speed before taking the inevitable plunge into the river. You're lucky if your only injury is embarrassment.

Jeff was sitting on a large rock in a shallow, sandy backwater pool talking to my son Lance as I came downstream. I sloshed through the knee-deep water until within 8 or 10 feet of them and then tripped over what was probably the only other rock in the pool; I paid homage to Jeff full-length, face down in the river. I wasn't in any danger, but was greatly concerned that either or both of them would die laughing.

If you're in thigh-deep or shallower water, the danger isn't that you won't be able to get out. The danger is that you'll break an arm, leg, ribs, or twist some part of your anatomy that will make getting out more difficult or impossible. There's also the distasteful possibility of hitting your head and drowning while you're unconscious. How much better to just accept the inevitable and sit down, with the only damage to your pride!

If you should fall in fairly deep fast water, forget the equipment! Yes, that rod and reel are dear to you, but you're dear to your friends and family; a few hundred dollars' worth of equipment isn't a fair exchange for your life. Try to get on your back with your feet downstream so you can see what's ahead, and aim yourself towards shallower water. Drag one hand under you, so that you can feel when the water gets shallow enough for you to gain some sort of hold.

One thing you can do to make your wading safer is to carry a wading staff. It's not exactly a third leg, but it does allow you to have two points (one foot and the staff) anchored when you take a step in the stream. I don't usually carry a staff (Don does), but there have been a few times when I was wishing desperately for one. There are a few places that I wouldn't venture into without having one along.

Wading Quietly

Nearly as important as wading safely is the need to wade quietly. Most of us had the experience as kids of putting our heads underwater and cracking two rocks together. We were amazed at how loud the sound was, amplified many times over what we'd hear in the air. Well, every rock that you roll into another in the stream creates a loud noise under water, and fish are very sensitive to sound vibrations.

One of the advantages of dry-fly fishing is that you're usually moving upstream in order to cast so that your fly drifts to the fish. This means that you're approaching the trout from behind, since they're facing upstream. Any noise that you make wading tends to be carried downstream, away from the fish. But a clumsy stumble creates a lot of disturbance and will often shut down feeding trout for quite a distance upstream.

When you are moving downstream (fishing streamers, for example), any sound vibrations that you create by sloppy wading tend to be carried down to the fish, so careful wading is even more critical. The only way to wade quietly is to wade slowly and carefully—it's also the safest way.

Wading Tips and Techniques

There's a stretch of the North Platte River in Wyoming called the Miracle Mile that gets a run of huge brown trout from the reservoir below it in the fall and another run of rainbows and cutthroats in the spring. It's a big river, with a heavy flow of water, and wading it can be treacherous. One stretch that we fish has a sandy shoreline. When you are out in the river only thigh deep or so, you can feel the sand washing out from under your feet— not an entirely comfortable feeling. There are some islands that offer access to parts of the river that you can't reach from the main shore. To get to those, you need to wade across knee-deep, very fast water. This is one of the few places where we always carry wading staffs—and not lightweight ones, either. Don takes a push broom handle, bores a hole in the bottom end, and epoxies a 10-inch-long (25 cm) piece of quarter-inch steel rod about halfway into the wood. He bores a hole near the top of the handle and strings a 3- or 4-foot-long (1 or 1.2 m) piece of parachute cord through it. The steel tip gives solid purchase on any bottom type and also weights the bottom end so that it's easier to get it firmly anchored in the current. The finished product is a staff you can have confidence in; it sure is mud ugly, though. He ties the loose end of the wading staff cord to a strap on his vest, and the staff just floats along downriver when he's fishing, but it is readily available when needed. I do the same.

A ski-pole wading staff. You can strip the basket off an old ski pole and use the pole as a wading staff. Some ski poles are pretty flimsy, though, and it's tough finding one that is long enough. (Your staff should be about up to your shoulder, or just a tad shorter.) A problem we've found with this kind of staff is that the pole is hollow and, of course, it wants to float. It's sometimes a bit of a struggle to get the bottom end to stay on the stream bed. It does make a pretty good, lightweight staff, however, and the price is right.

Aluminum wading staffs. There are some wading staffs on the market that are made of several sections of aluminum tubing strung together with bungee cord. They fold up into a neat pouch on your wading belt and spring into a one-piece staff when removed from the pouch. The standard model is a little too short for most people, but they make a heavy-duty model that is longer and made from heavier tubing. The only disadvantage to the heavy-duty model is that, being hollow, it wants to float. It's difficult to get the bottom end to stay down in the stream bed. If you turn the staff upside down and pull off the rubber crutch tip on the bottom end, you can insert a plug about 2 inches (5 cm) up in the tubing, fill it up with lead shot, and put the crutch tip back on. Then the bottom end will go to the bottom of the stream bed and stay put.

Don't wade when false-casting or when your fly is drifting. There are two times when you shouldn't be moving in the stream: when you're casting and during the drift following your cast. Trying to wade while false-casting usually results in messing up both operations. Either you stumble, disrupting the timing of your cast and wrapping the line and leader around the rod, or you don't devote enough attention to wading and you trip over a rock.

I've finally learned not to wade while my fly is still making its drift. Trout almost seem to have an instinct that tells them when you're taking a step, and that's when they take your fly. Boy, is that fun to watch!

The safest method is to fish out a drift and simply let the line trail downstream as you wade a few steps to your new position. If it's tricky water to wade, if you're getting out of the stream, or if you're going to wade some distance, you're better off reeling in your line and then wading.

Slide your feet. In a rocky stream, the best wading technique is to slide your feet along, one at a time. This gives you an opportunity to feel your way with one foot while you are still firmly planted on the other. There's a trap here, though: sometimes you'll slide your foot up under the edge of a rock without knowing it. You slide the other foot to a firm hold, and then, as you step forward, the foot that's under the rock catches and pulls you back into a wet landing. Wading slowly and methodically is the solution.

Wiggle your feet to avoid sinking. Wiggle your feet around occasionally when you are wading in a section of stream with a sand or mud bottom. When you try to move, you don't want to find that you've sunk in to the point that you can't get your foot out.

If you do get stuck, lifting your leg isn't much help if you have boot-foot waders on, because your foot simply comes up out of the boot into the leg of the wader. You can help a lot by lifting the leg of the wader with your hand(s). Sometimes you'll have to work one foot partway out and then shift your weight to that foot while your work the other foot partway out, and so on, until you're free. The best bet is to check frequently that you can move your feet *before* you get stuck.

Wear a glasses holder. A fall into the river will almost always result in your eyeglasses or sunglasses coming off. Not only are they expensive to replace, you're not going to be able to fish very well without them; some of us would have trouble finding the car in an open field without them. You may lose most of a day's fishing while you stop to get them replaced. The solution is to wear a cord of some kind on your glasses. There are many nice ones on the market, and they're inexpensive. In a pinch, a piece of tippet material looped behind your neck and tied to each temple piece will keep you from losing your glasses if you fall or stumble.

Wade at an angle. It's much easier to wade up- or downstream at an angle, rather than straight across or directly into or with the current, as you present less of your body to the current at an angle. For the same reason, it's less tiring to stand in the current when you are turned sideways to it.

Turning around. One of the trickiest moments in wading is when you need to turn around. You double or triple the amount of your body exposed to the force of the current as you turn to face upstream or downstream, and the force can literally bowl you over. You need to increase your lean into the current as you turn and present more of your body to the force of the current.

Felt-soled waders. Felt-soled waders are great for wading in rivers full of slippery rocks, but be careful when you get out of the stream—they're like skis on wet grass or in the mud along the bank.

Walk or watch—not both. You don't have to be in the water to take a nasty fall. We all have the tendency to watch the stream for rises or other indications of our quarry while we're walking along the bank; it's a good way to trip and fall. The solution is much as when you're in the water. Either walk or watch; doing both simultaneously is dangerous.

Phil Camera

Crossing a heavy current. Crossing a river with heavy current can be extremely dangerous. Some tips to remember are:

- Tighten your wading belt before starting.
- Use a wading staff strong enough to support your body weight.

- Present minimum body surface area to the water flow—wade with the front of your body at 90 degrees to the current.
- If the water pushes your feet downstream when you are trying to wade across, go back.
- If the water is washing sand from under your feet, go back.
- When crossing with a friend, cross side by side, with the stronger of the two people upstream. This allows the person on the down-stream side to wade in less current.

Get advice about unfamiliar streams. When wading in unfamiliar streams, it's wise to ask local residents about any dangerous conditions that may occur, such as:

- An extremely slippery bottom
- Unannounced releases of water from an upstream dam
- The presence of poisonous snakes
- Whether the way in is the only way back out.

Inflatable vest. One of the best safety tips I know when wading in heavy water and big rivers is to wear an inflatable vest under your fishing vest. If you were to slip in heavy, fast water, the inflatable vest could mean the difference between life and death.

Al Diem

Practice falling in. The only way to really get comfortable with falling in is to do it—but do it under controlled conditions. A swimming pool is ideal for the exercise: put on your waders and vest, get a rod (preferably not your grandfather's Leonard bamboo), and jump in where it's just deep enough to stand up. Now, the first thing to do is get rid of the rod. Try to roll over on your back (just as if you were going downriver), and then get your feet under you and stand up. Next, try to walk up into the shallower water and get out. Not very pleasant, huh? Now visualize what it must be like when you're being carried downstream by a fast current. At least you now have an idea of what to expect if it happens for real. I'll also bet you'll wade more carefully from now on. By the way, pick a pool with some privacy for the exercise, because you're going to look pretty ridiculous. A shallow pond or a quiet pool in a river can, of course, also be used.

Get the air out of your waders. Your waders will fit better and will present less resistance to the river flow if you'll get into a quiet, waist-deep area, loosen your wading belt, and squat down in the water. The water pressure will force most of the air out of your waders; then you can fasten or tighten your wading belt.

Jerry Gibbs

When to avoid wading. Sometimes the best fishing afoot requires no wading at all. This is especially true on small, brushy streams where poking through the bankside growth and simply flipping—not casting—a fly into pockets and runs is most productive. You'll also avoid damaging a small, fragile ecosystem by tromping through it.

Joan Wulff

Where to look. When wading, look ahead to where you will move your forward foot but, as you move it, don't look down. You may get vertigo. Focus instead on another spot farther away.

Waterproof watch. It's easy to trip or slip when you're wading. I finally bought a "fishing watch," one that can take submersion; this, along with my waterproof camera, has allowed me to fall in with less worry. The problem then becomes one of lost dignity. The first thing you do when you are back on your feet is look around to see who was watching.

chapter six

Miscellany

Tips and Techniques

Airplane carry-on baggage. When you're flying somewhere for a fishing trip, your carry-on bag should include your vest (with reel and fly boxes), your waders and wading shoes, toiletry kit, and a change of underwear. Carry one of your rods with you as carry-on baggage and, for heaven's sake, don't forget to get it from the flight attendants before deplaning, because they will have put it in the coat closest. You can get by for a long while in the same clothes if you have to, but your trip will be ruined if you have to wait two or three days for your fishing equipment. Equipment is too expensive for most of us to duplicate at the destination, even if it is available.

Waterproof camera. If you are serious about recording your fishing adventures on film, consider buying yourself a waterproof camera. You can get one for less than the price of a good graphite rod. You'll find that you'll be much more likely to take it along, since you don't have to be concerned about carrying it in your vest.

Protect your wallet and camera. A plastic zip-closure bag is good insurance for keeping your wallet and all its contents dry if you should fall while wading. It'll also work for carrying along a non-waterproof camera.

New-style rod cases. The new-style rod cases, which allow you to put your rod away with the reel attached, are really handy. Most of them have one or two fabric-covered plastic tubes inside a heavy Cordura shell. If you leave these cases leaning against your vehicle out in the sun, they will develop not-so-nice curves by the time you get back from a few hours of fishing. Lay the cases flat in your vehicle when you go to the river.

They all have very soft liners around the tubes to protect your rod and reel, so make sure that the equipment is dry before storing them away. That soft fabric will absorb the moisture from a wet rod and reel and create a real humidor, great for storing cigars, but not good for your prized fishing tackle.

Medications. I know of a fellow who had his bags searched at customs. They found an assortment of pills in a film canister. They were all over-the-counter drugs. He had simply thrown a few aspirin, decongestants, and the like in the container to save space. Since they weren't in their original packaging, he was held up for several hours until customs could have them tested (at his expense) to see what they were.

If you need to take along any medications when traveling out of the country, make sure they are in their original containers with the pharmacy label still on. It's a good idea to carry a copy of any prescriptions along with you in case you need further proof that what you have is a valid prescription for your use.

Teaching time. If you're taking a youngster (or an adult, for that matter) out to teach him or her to flyfish, then focus on that goal. You can't fish and teach another person at the same time. If you try to fish and teach, you'll both end up frustrated, if not angry. Either *take* the beginner fishing or *you go* fishing. There'll be time later to share the stream when the person you're teaching is accomplished enough to not need your constant attention.

A crush-proof rod case. I was flying in to a remote camp in Alaska with a group of clients for a one-week flyfishing school. We arrived in Dillingham for the transfer to the float plane when we saw our luggage for the first time since we started out. One man's aluminum rod case had obviously been run over by a baggage cart or some sort of vehicle. A section about 6 inches wide in the middle of the case was completely flattened. We assumed the rod was destroyed, but we couldn't

even get it out of the case to check. The airlines did replace it—three or four weeks after he returned home. Fortunately, I had a couple of spare rods with me, so his trip wasn't ruined.

Here's the formula for a travel case that even the airline baggage gorillas can't destroy. Go down to your local hardware and buy an appropriate length of 1½-inch schedule 40 PVC. It's about three times as thick as the polyurethane tubing used for rod cases, and it's hard. Tell them you need a cap, a PVC-to-pipe thread adapter, and a threaded cap for the adapter. You'll also need to get a small can of PVC cleaner and cement.

When you get home, cut a small circle of soft foam and fit it inside the cap. Clean the tube and the inside of the cap with the cleaner, and cement the cap on one end of the tube. Clean and cement the adapter on the other end, put your name and address on the tube with a permanent marker, and you're ready to go. It's heavy and it's ugly as sin, but it can take on anything the airlines can dish out, including being run over by a baggage cart.

Phil Camera

Research your trip. I've found that the more information I have about a new fishing destination, the better the trip will be. One of the best ways to research a trip is through periodicals and source books. A good one is *The Trout Fishing Source Book* by Mark D.

William. This book gives the names and addresses of state regulatory authorities and departments and guides, and lists reference books for nearly all areas. A book of this type is invaluable in your fishing library.

Jerry Gibbs

Flash photos. A lot of fishing trip photos are disappointing because of dark shadows across the angler's face cast by a hat brim. Avoid this by using a flash to fill in those shadows—especially when there's a bright sun overhead.

Avoid distortion. If your fishing camera has a lens wider than 35 mm, you can distort people in your photos, causing heads to elongate and noses to appear to grow large. To avoid the problem, don't tilt the camera up or down when taking the photo. Keep it parallel to your subject by raising or lowering yourself as necessary to compose the picture.

Transporting reels. I've never had a problem transporting fly reels in big duffels once they were packed in their individual padded bags and placed inside a specialized reel case. But you'll feel better with your prime reels in a carry-on bag.

Magnetic rod racks. Those magnetic rod racks that allow you to carry your fully rigged rods on your car hood, swept back over the roof, are sweet when spot-hopping along rivers. Just make sure to keep a reel bag on for protection, and watch for overhanging tree branches.

Watch your carry-on equipment. One of the great moments of danger for prized carry-on equipment (and your personal papers and gear) occurs just before the final transfer to a fishing camp/lodge. Typically, you are greeted by a representative of the operation while the staff loads mountains of gear for the final leg in. Keep a sharp eye on your carry-on goods. It's very easy for them to wind up with the rest of the bulk equipment—maybe even crushed beneath the heavy stuff.

Glossary

Here's a list of common terms that you're likely to run across in this book and in other flyfishing literature. You'll certainly recognize some of the words, but flyfishing does have a language of its own. Some words have a peculiar meaning in the context of the sport.

Action: A general term used to describe the feel and response of a fly rod (soft, stiff, slow, intermediate, or fast action).

Adult: The mature stage in the life cycle of an insect.

Alderfly: A member of the insect order Megaloptera; undergoes complete metamorphosis.

Artic grayling (*Thymallus arcticus*): Not a true trout or char, but a member of the salmonid family, characterized by its bright coloration and large dorsal fin.

Artificial: A type of fly made to imitate a living insect.

Attractor: A fly that is not tied to represent a specific food form.

Automatic reel: A fly reel in which a spring is wound as the line is stripped; the action of the spring then retrieves the line.

Backcast: That portion of the fly cast in which the line moves into the area behind the angler.

Backing: Line tied between the reel spool and the fly line, used to help fill the spool (increasing the retrieving speed), to attach the line to the spool, and to provide extra line for fighting large fish.

Balance: Line, rod, and reel in a combination that results in an efficient system for flycasting.

Bamboo: A tropical grass (Tonkin cane) whose stem is used in the construction of fly rods.

Barb: A raised nick cut out of the point of a hook, so that once it penetrates, it can't return through the puncture.

Barbless hook: A hook made without a barb, or a hook with the barb removed or flattened.

Barrel knot: A knot used to join two pieces of monofilament of nearly equal diameters, also called a blood knot.

Bead-head: A fly tied with a glass or metal bead just behind the hook eye.

Beetle: Common name for members of the insect order Coleoptera. Both aquatic and terrestrial beetles may be important to the flyfisher.

Belly: The sagging portion of a fly line, whether in the air or on the water.

Bend: The curved section at the rear of a hook.

Blood knot: A knot used for joining two pieces of monofilament of nearly equal diameters, particularly sections of leader material; also called a barrel knot.

Brook trout (*Salvelinus fontinalis*): A member of the Salmonidae family, but a char. Chars have different dentition than other trout.

Brown trout (*Salmo trutta*): A true trout and one of the flyfisher's favorite quarries.

Bucktail: A streamer fly tied with a wing constructed from the tail hair of a whitetail deer.

Caddis (or caddisfly): A member of the insect order Trichoptera. Caddisflies undergo complete metamorphosis. The caddis is one of the most important insects in the diet of most trout and therefore is of great importance to the flyfisher.

Cane rod: Another name for a bamboo rod.

Cased caddis: Any of the species of caddis that live in a case during the larval and pupal stages.

Cast: (1) (v.) The act of moving the fly line in the air. (2) (n.)Two or more flies attached to the same leader for presentation to the trout (as in "a cast of flies").

Chest waders: Waders that come up to the top of the chest of the wearer.

Clinch knot: A knot commonly used to attach the fly to the leader tippet.

Coleoptera: The order of insects that includes all of the beetles.

Complete metamorphosis: The life cycle of insects that pass through four distinct stages: egg, larva, pupa, and adult.

Complex hatch: The simultaneous hatching of several types and/or species of aquatic insects.

Compound hatch: A complex hatch in which a hatch of smaller insects is hidden or masked by the hatching of larger insects.

Crane fly: An insect of the order Diptera, family Tipulidae, which in the adult stage resembles a large mosquito. There are both aquatic and terrestrial crane flies. Crane flies undergo complete metamorphosis.

Curve cast: A cast in which the angler causes the fly and leader to land either left or right of the fly line.

Cutthroat trout *(Onchorhynchus clarki):* A true trout, found mostly in the western United States.

Damselfly: A large aquatic insect of the order Odonata, suborder Zygoptera, that resembles its close relative, the dragonfly.

Dapping: A fishing technique in which the fly is repeatedly bounced on and off the surface of the water.

Dead drift: A method of presenting the fly in which no motion is imparted to the fly by the angler.

Diptera: An order of insects whose members have two wings and undergo complete metamorphosis. Midges, mosquitoes, houseflies, black flies, and crane flies are Diptera.

Dobson fly: Large insects of the order Megaloptera. They undergo complete metamorphosis. Their nymphs, which are commonly called hellgrammites, resemble stoneflies.

Dolly Varden *(Salvelinus malma):* A char, although commonly called Dolly Varden trout; may actually be a subspecies of the Arctic char.

Double-haul: A casting stroke in which additional force is imparted to the rod and the beginning of both the forward and back casts by sharply pulling the line with the line hand.

Double-tapered line: A fly line that is heaviest in the center and tapers equally towards each end.

Downstream: In the direction of the water's flow.

Drag: The force of the water against the line or leader which causes the fly to move unnaturally in or on the water; also, the mechanical system in a reel that applies friction to the spool.

Dragonfly: A large aquatic insect of the order Odonata, suborder Anisoptera, which resembles its close relative the damselfly. Dragonflies undergo incomplete metamorphosis.

Drake: A common term for the adult male mayfly.

Dropper: The secondary fly or flies attached to the leader in a cast of flies.

Dry fly: A fly that is tied to represent the adult stage of an insect and designed to float on the surface of the water.

Dun: (1) A common term for the subimago, or first winged stage, of the adult mayfly. (2) A neutral, slightly brownish dark grey color.

Emerger: A term used loosely to describe any insect that moves up towards the surface of the water preparatory to hatching into the adult stage.

Entomology: The formal study of insects.

Ephemeroptera: The order of insects comprising the mayflies; they undergo incomplete metamorphosis, but are unique in that they have two adult stages: subimago (dun) and imago (spinner).

False cast: A series of forward and back casts in which the line is kept in the air; used to adjust line length and dry the fly.

Feeding: The active taking of food by fish.

Feeding lane: A narrow strip of current that carries food to a trout's feeding lie.

Feeding lie: The position in the stream that a trout moves into to feed.

Felt soles: Soles originally made of wool felt applied to the soles of waders or wading shoes to provide traction on moss- or algae-covered rocks. Generally, wool felt has been replaced by synthetic materials.

Ferrule: Originally, the male and female metal pieces used to join two sections of a rod; now used to refer to the connection itself, even if one rod section fits into the other without metal connectors.

Float: The action of a dry fly on the water (e.g., a drag-free float, a long float).

Floatant: A substance applied to a line, fly, or leader to assist it in floating.

Floating line: A fly line designed and built to float on the surface of the water.

Float tube: A fabric seat attached to an innertube-like flotation device, which enables the angler to float on the surface of the water; also called a belly boat.

Fly: An arrangement of materials on a hook, meant to entice a fish.

Fly box: A container designed specifically for storing and carrying flies.

Forceps: A small pliers-like tool that locks closed; it assists the angler in holding small items and in removing the fly from a fish.

Forward cast: That portion of a fly cast in which the line is in front of the caster.

Free-living: Description of caddis species that don't build permanent cases during the larval stage.

Freestone streams: Tumbling, fast-moving streams, usually with rock-covered bottoms. They are subject to extreme changes in depth and speed of water flow, because they are formed from an accumulation of trickles from small springs, snow melt, or rainfall, which originate at higher elevations.

Free-swimming: Caddis species that don't build permanent cases during the larval stage; same as *free-living*.

Freshwater shrimp: Small aquatic crustaceans that are a prime food source for trout in some areas, primarily lakes and their tailwaters.

Gap: The distance between the shank and point of a hook. Hook size is only an indication of the gap of the hook.

Golden trout (*Onchorhyncus aquabonita*): A beautiful trout native only to the Mt. Whitney area in California; it has been transplanted, but is normally found only at elevations above 8,000 feet (2461 m).

Grannom: A common name for the caddisfly.

Graphite: A mineral and also a man-made material consisting of carbon fibers. Synthetic graphite is used in the manufacture of strong, lightweight fly rods.

Greased: Treated with floatant.

Grip: The handle of the rod; also, the hand position used in holding the rod.

Guides: The devices on a rod through which the line runs.

Hair-winged: Having wings made of hair instead of feathers, as in a hair-winged fly.

Hand-retrieve: Line retrieval technique in which the line is alternately picked up between the thumb and forefinger and then between the thumb and little finger, forming loops held in the hand.

Hatch: (1) (v.) The transformation of an aquatic insect into its adult form. (2) (n.) A large number of aquatic insects that emerge over a short period of time (e.g., a hatch of caddisflies).

Hen: A female insect; normally used in reference to mayflies.

High-density line: A sinking fly line built so that its density is much greater than 1 (the density of water), so it sinks very fast.

Hip boots: Waterproof boots whose tops come to the wearer's thighs.

Hippers: Another name for hip boots.

Holding lie: Where a trout normally remains when not feeding; also called a resting lie.

Hook-keeper: A small hook or eyelet mounted on a fly rod, just forward of the handle, where a fly can be hooked when not being cast.

Imago: (1) The second, and last, adult stage in the life cycle of a mayfly, at which time it is also called a spinner. (2) An insect in its final adult, sexually mature, usually winged stage.

Imitation: A fly tied to represent realistically a particular food form.

Improved clinch knot: Same as the clinch knot, but with the tag end passed back through the knot before tightening, to prevent the knot from slipping.

Incomplete metamorphosis: The life cycle of insects that pass through only three stages: egg, nymph, and adult.

Instar: A stage in the larval development of an insect between two successive molts.

Knotless leader: A leader whose smooth taper is formed during the manufacturing process.

Knotted leader: A leader whose taper is formed by tying together monofilament lengths of decreasing diameters.

Larva: The stage between the egg and pupa in the life cycle of an insect that undergoes complete metamorphosis.

Leader: A section of monofilament line, usually tapered, that is attached to the end of the fly line and to which the fly is tied.

Leader sink: Any of several materials used to treat a leader so that it will break the surface tension and sink below the surface of the water.

Leader straightener: A double-sided pad, usually lined with rubber, through which the leader is drawn to take out any kinks.

Leech: Carnivorous or blood-sucking annelid worms that inhabit most lakes; a common trout food.

Level line: A fly line constructed with the same diameter from end to end.

Lie: A particular spot where a trout may be found (a holding lie, a feeding lie, a primary lie).

Life cycle: The stages of development of an insect (or other living thing) from egg to adult.

Line hand: The hand not holding the rod when casting.

Line weight: A designation of the weight of a fly line, based on the weight of the first 30 feet (9.2 m) of line.

Loop: The candy-cane shape that a fly line takes during the casting stroke.

Loop control: The manner in which the shape of the loop is formed during the cast (e.g., a wide loop, a tight loop).

Marabou streamer: A streamer fly tied using marabou feathers as the wing.

Masking hatch: The emergence of adult aquatic insects of a large, brightly colored species that hides the fact that a smaller species is present.

Mayfly: An aquatic insect of the order Ephemeroptera; a primary trout food.

Mend: The act of controlling the fly line on the water; usually the motion of flipping the belly of the line upstream.

Metamorphosis: A series of changes in the physical form of a developing insect (or other animal). Complete metamorphosis consists of egg, larva, pupa, and adult. Incomplete metamorphosis consists of the egg, nymph, and adult stages only.

Midge: The common name for some groups of very small insects of the order Diptera; also, a term used for any small insect or fly used to imitate a tiny insect.

Midge rod: A short, lightweight rod.

Mosquito: A member of the insect order Diptera, family Culicidae.

Nail knot: The most common knot used for attaching the butt of the leader to the fly line; also called a needle knot.

Natural: (n.) A living insect, as opposed to an artificial fishing fly.

Net: A circular or oval frame with an open-weave bag attached, used to land a hooked fish; also called a landing net.

Nippers: Another term for clippers, used to closely trim the tag ends of line after knots are tied.

No-hackle fly: A type of dry fly, popularized by Swisher and Richards, which doesn't use hackle as the support for the floating fly.

No-kill: A rule or an individual's philosophy whereby all fish are returned to the water unharmed.

Nymph: (1) The stage between the egg and adult in the life cycle of an insect that undergoes incomplete metamorphosis. (2) Any artificial fly that is imitative of any underwater stage (nymph, larva, or pupa) of various insects. For example, even though a caddisfly doesn't have a nymphal stage, the flies that imitate this insect's underwater forms are often referred to as nymphs.

Nymphing: Any of various fishing methods in which the angler presents an imitation of an underwater stage of an insect.

Odonata: An order of insects that includes dragonflies and damselflies; they undergo incomplete metamorphosis.

Onchorhyncus aquabonita: The scientific name for golden trout.

Onchorhyncus clarki: The scientific name for cutthroat trout.

Onchorhyncus mykiss: The scientific name for rainbow trout.

Oviposit: The act of laying eggs, particularly among insects.

Periwinkle: A colloquial term for cased caddis larva or pupa.

Plecoptera: An order of insects commonly called stoneflies. They undergo incomplete metamorphosis.

Pocket water: A section of water whose surface is mostly broken, but contains some small areas (or pockets) of smooth water.

Poly-wing: A dry fly tied using polypropylene yarn for the wing.

Pool: A section of slow-moving water whose surface is unbroken.

Presentation: The method of placing a fly where a fish is most likely to see it in a natural manner; includes the manner in which the cast is completed and the method in which the fly is fished.

Pupa: The stage between the larval and adult stages of an insect that undergoes complete metamorphosis.

Rainbow trout (*Onchorhyncus mykiss*): A true trout and one of the species most sought after by the fly-fisher.

Reach cast: A line presentation method in which the rod is moved left or right at the completion of the cast before the line falls to the water. Used to move the belly of the line upstream to increase the length of the drag-free float of the fly.

Reel seat: The mechanism on the rod that holds the reel in place.

Retrieve: (n.) Any of several techniques used to bring the line in after the completion of a cast; sometimes used to impart motion to a fly.

Reverse cast: A casting technique in which the angler aims the forward cast away from the stream into an open space in the trees or brush and then turns to face the stream to complete the cast to the water.

Rise: The act of the fish taking an insect from the surface of the water.

Rise form: The surface disturbance created by a rise.

Rock worm: A colloquial term for a caddis larva or pupa (probably because many species build their cases of small stones); also, the larval stage of the crane fly (family Tipulidae).

Roll cast: A casting method in which the line slides across the water towards the caster and then leaves the water in a forward rolling motion.

Run: A particular stretch of moving water (e.g., the run below the home pool).

Running line: Another term for backing, particularly when used in reference to the backing attached to a shooting head.

Runoff: The high water resulting from either early summer snow melt or recent rains.

Salmon flies: Flies tied specifically for salmon fishing; a colloquial term for stonefly adults, especially *Pteronarcys californica.*

Salmo trutta: The scientific name for brown trout.

Salvelinus fontinalis: The scientific name for brook trout (a char).

Salvelinus malma: The scientific name for Dolly Varden trout (a char).

S-cast: A casting technique in which the caster moves the rod tip from side to side at the completion of the forward cast so that the line lands on the water in a series of small curves; used to create slack in the line to resist drag.

Serpentine cast: Another term for the S-cast.

Shooting: A casting technique in which the weight of a short section of line is used to pull a longer section of line behind it at the completion of the forward cast; often used when there is no room for a sufficient backcast or when a very long cast must be made.

Shooting basket: A small basket that can be attached to the waist to hold loose line so that it can be cast by the shooting method.

Shooting head: A type of fly line designed to be used with the shooting method of casting, normally only 30 feet long.

Simple hatch: The emergence of only one species of aquatic insect.

Single-action reel: A fly reel that applies the same amount of drag on the line when stripping line or winding it in.

Sinking line: A fly line designed with a density greater than water, so that it will sink effectively.

Sink rate: The speed at which a sinking line descends through the water.

Slack-line cast: Any of several types of casts that end with slack line on the water.

Snake cast: Another term for the S-cast or serpentine cast.

Spate: High water; also, a stream is said to be "in spate" when the water is higher than normal.

Spent: Exhausted or dead; usually applied to a dead insect floating on the water.

Spent-wing: An insect whose wings are lying out in a horizontal position, normally as a result of death.

Split shot: A small ball of lead with a slit cut into it so it can be pinched onto the leader to sink the leader.

Steelhead trout: A sea-run rainbow trout.

Stillborn flies: Insects that were malformed or otherwise unable to enter completely into the adult stage when hatching.

Stonefly: A member of the insect order Plecoptera.

Stop cast: A casting technique in which extra force is applied to the forward cast and then the rod is suddenly stopped as the line straightens, so that it bounces back towards the caster and falls to the water in a series of curves.

Streamer: A fly tied to imitate a small minnow or baitfish.

Strike indicator: A small piece of floating material attached to the leader to assist the nymph fisher in detecting when a fish has taken the fly.

Stripping: The act of retrieving line; also, the act of pulling line from the reel.

Taper: The shape of a fly line from end to end; e.g., a forward taper line, a double-taper line. Also, a tapered leader is sometimes called a taper.

Terrestrial: Of or relating to an insect whose life cycle is completed outside of the aquatic environment.

Upstream: In the direction opposite to the flow of the water.

Waders: Another term for chest waders.

Wading sandals: Sandals designed to be worn on rubber-soled hippers or waders to provide better traction through the use of felt soles or metal cleats.

Wading shoes: Shoes worn over stocking-foot waders.

Wading staff: A sturdy staff used to assist in wading.

Weighted flies: Flies that are weighted with lead so that they will sink quickly.

Weight-forward line: A fly line whose heavier section has been moved towards the forward end of the line.

Wet fly: A fly that is fished below the surface, generally in imitation of an emerging insect.

Wind knot: Overhand knots that occur in the leader as a result of an improper casting stroke.

Zygoptera: The suborder of insects of the order Odonata that includes the dragonflies and damselflies.

Equipment and Supply Checklists

For a One-Day Outing

Rod
Reel
Waders/Hippers
Wading Shoes
Gaiters

Fly Vest or Chest Pack with contents given below:
- Fly boxes
- Spare leader
- Clippers
- Leader straightener
- Polarized sunglasses
- Forceps
- Hook-sharpening stone
- Tippet spools: sizes 3, 4, 5, and 6X
- Desiccant
- Floatant
- Leader sink
- Weights
- Strike indicators
- Insect repellent
- Safety pin
- Rain jacket
- Spare car keys
- Fishing license

Trip Bag containing the following:
- Spare socks
- First-aid kit: aspirin, plastic bandages, decongestant, antacid tablets, antiseptic cream
- Sunscreen
- Mini-flashlight
- Spare tip guide
- Super Glue
- Fly stock box
- Line cleaner
- Wader patch kit
- Trout stomach pump
- Stream thermometer
- Mini-screwdriver set
- Multi-tool (Leatherman, Gerber, or similar)
- Sweater (seasonal)
- Lunch
- Empty 35-mm film canisters
- Emery paper
- Hard-as-Nails fingernail hardener
- Gloves (seasonal)
- Spare reel spools/lines

For a Multi-Day Outing

Follow the lists given above, but add:
- Clothes as appropriate
- Toiletry kit
- Flytying kit
- Spare rod
- Spare reel
- Additional leaders
- Sleeping bag and camping equipment (if needed)

Metric Conversion Chart

inches	cm	inches	cm	inches	cm
1/8	0.3	4	10.2	17	43.2
1/4	0.6	4 1/2	11.4	18	45.7
3/8	1.0	5	12.7	19	48.3
1/2	1.3	6	15.2	20	50.8
5/8	1.6	7	17.8	21	53.3
3/4	1.9	8	20.3	22	55.9
7/8	2.2	9	22.9	23	58.4
1	2.5	10	25.4	24	61.0
1 1/4	3.2	11	27.9	25	63.5
1 1/2	3.8	12	30.5	26	66.0
2	5.1	13	33.0	27	68.6
2 1/2	6.4	14	35.6	28	71.1
3	7.6	15	38.1	29	73.7
3 1/2	8.9	16	40.6	30	76.2

Index